Useful Tips, Hints, and Shortcuts & INDEX

WOMAN ALIVE

Useful Tips, Hints, and Shortcuts & INDEX

Aldus Books London

Series Coordinator: John Mason
Design Director: Guenther Radtke
Picture Editor: Peter Cook
Editor: Susan Allen
Copy Editor: Mitzi Bales
Research: Nina Sklansky
Consultants: Beppie Harrison
　　　　　　 Jo Sandilands

Copyright © Aldus Books Limited,
London, 1974
Library of Congress Catalog Card
No. 72–85024
Printed and bound in Yugoslavia by
Mladinska Knjiga, Ljubljana

Contents

Almost everything that you may have to do can usually be done in some quicker, cheaper, or easier way – from peeling onions to getting the last drop out of the ketchup bottle, from taking care of a pet to giving a party for your children. It's all in the knowing how, and the first part of this book will tell you how. In it you'll find many useful tips and hints on such varied and interesting topics as entertaining, furniture repair, housekeeping, gardening, and etiquette for children. By making imagination count more than dollars, and by helping you to be more inventive, this book will become one of your handiest references. In addition, starting on page 63 is the full index to all the Woman Alive books – a quick guide to whatever you want to look up.

For Better Management	6
A Pet in the House	10
Furniture Fix-ups	18
What Sticks What?	21
Remove that Stain!	22
Entertainingly Yours	25
The Table Beautiful	30
Drinks and Wine	36
Mixing Drinks	38
Party Punches	40
A Guide to Food & Wine	41
The Wedding: Who Pays for What?	42
Party Fun for Kids	44
Children's Etiquette	47
Making the Garden Grow	50
General Tips, Hints, and Shortcuts	56
Woman Alive Index	63

For Better Management

Wise food buying is one of the important—and necessary—ways to economize these days. A tip to remember : do your comparison shopping.

There are hundreds of little ways you can save time, money, and energy in housekeeping, especially in the cooking, baking, shopping, and storing of food. This section gives you some homemaking ideas that are new, others that are tried-and-true, all that are useful in helping you get more done in less time at lower cost. You'll refer to it often for just that right helpful hint you need.

☐ Foods stacked prominently at the end of a supermarket aisle are presumed to be specials by many shoppers. Not necessarily. Before you grab a can or package from these stacks, check the price.

☐ Nonfood items, such as paper towels, soaps, and household cleaners, add up to a hefty 20 per cent or more of the average grocery bill. In most areas of the country, there is a good chance you can buy these items more cheaply in discount stores.

☐ Water is the extra ingredient you're paying for in those heat-and-serve soups. Buy condensed soups and add the water yourself.

☐ Don't stuff leftovers into odd corners of the

refrigerator. Keep them all on one shelf, or on one side. In this way you can keep track of what you are accumulating, and use the leftovers before they go bad.

☐ To save as much as possible of a burned food, uncover the pan, and set it in a bigger pot of cold water until all the steam has escaped. Much of the burned taste will pass off with the steam.

☐ Put a new powder puff in your canister of flour, and use it to dust flour into greased cake pans. Easier, faster, less wasteful.

☐ Put two sets of measuring spoons on the same ring. When using them for both wet and dry measures in the same recipe, you won't have to stop in the middle to wash one.

☐ If the counter space is short in your kitchen, place a cutting board over an open drawer, and you'll gain a little extra space.

☐ Many large bakeries run surplus or "day old" shops. Call the main plant of a bakery in your area, and ask if one is located near you. Buy in these shops for excellent savings.

☐ Stale cake can be freshened by placing it in a strainer over a pot of boiling water until it is moist and soft again.

☐ Stale bread can be made into crumbs by breaking it into chunks, and putting it in the blender for a few seconds. Store in a plastic bag in the freezer or refrigerator.

☐ To keep macaroni from boiling over, put about a tablespoon of oil in the water.

☐ A cheaper substitute for coffee cream—and one with fewer calories—can be made with two tablespoons of nonfat dry milk in a cup of whole milk.

☐ Evaporated milk, whipped and chilled, can be used in recipes calling for whipped cream.

☐ In recipes calling for ricotta cheese, use less expensive cottage cheese instead.

☐ Before boiling milk, rinse the pan in cold water. This will keep the milk from sticking to the pan.

☐ Sour milk should not be discarded. Use it in pancakes. They will be tasty and light. There are also many sour milk cake recipes.

☐ Wrapping cheese loosely will minimize the chance of its developing mold.

☐ Hard cheeses can be frozen for about three months, so store leftover bits until you have enough to use for cooking.

☐ Cheeses that have become dry can be grated and used in cooking. Mold that forms on cheeses can be scraped away—it will not damage the flavor or texture.

☐ Rub oil or margarine over the shell of very fresh eggs to keep them fresh longer. Be sure the entire shell is coated.

☐ Buy frozen vegetables that come in clear plastic bags rather than cartons. Not only can you see what you're buying, but you can also see how much you're using if you want to cook only part of the contents. Don't pick out your frozen foods until just before you head for the checkout counter; they will be less likely to defrost by the time you get home.

☐ Cut off the tops of carrots, beets, turnips, and parsnips before you store them in the

This chart shows how long canned goods can be kept without spoilage before you have to use them.

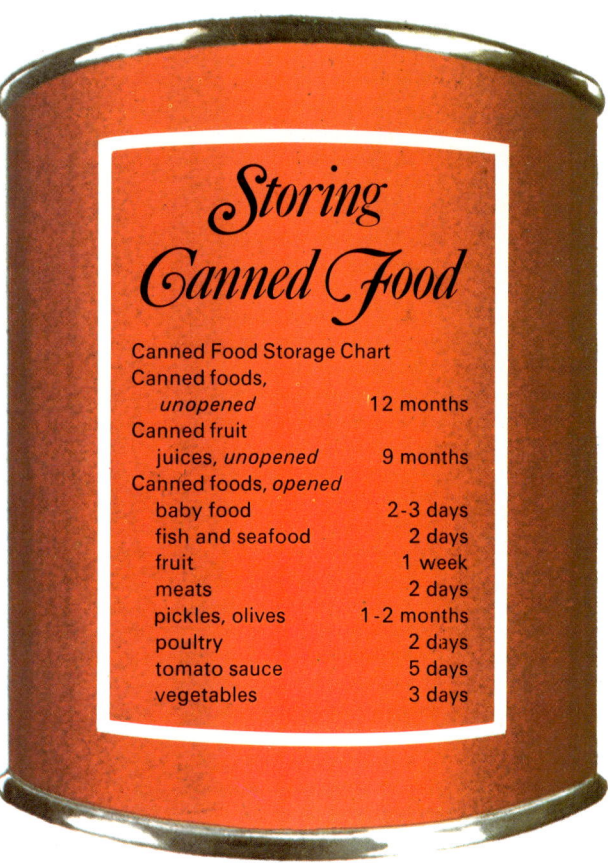

Storing Canned Food

Canned Food Storage Chart

Canned foods,	
unopened	12 months
Canned fruit	
juices, *unopened*	9 months
Canned foods, *opened*	
baby food	2-3 days
fish and seafood	2 days
fruit	1 week
meats	2 days
pickles, olives	1-2 months
poultry	2 days
tomato sauce	5 days
vegetables	3 days

refrigerator. If left on, the tops will draw off moisture and some of the food value of the roots.

☐ Spinach, escarole, chicory, and romaine are often cheaper than iceberg lettuce, and are much better sources of vitamin A.

☐ Don't wash fruits and vegetables until just before you use them. Moisture that may remain after washing encourages mold and rot.

☐ To prevent canned asparagus tips from breaking off, open the can and remove the vegetable from the bottom instead of the top.

☐ To keep onions from making your eyes tear, put a small chunk of bread on the end of your paring knife. The bread will absorb the juices and fumes of the onion.

☐ To bake potatoes in about half the time they normally take, parboil them for five minutes first. Drain and dry them before putting them in the oven.

☐ To get the most juice from lemons, let the skin start to shrivel a bit before you squeeze them.

☐ Save the rinds of squeezed lemons and oranges, and freeze them. They will be useful for cakes, frostings, and puddings, and are easier to grate when frozen. Peels may also be candied.

☐ Grating an orange or lemon too hard will give a bitter flavor to the food. The colored layer of the skin is the part that will give the flavor without bitterness, so grate lightly.

☐ Liquid left in pickle jars can be used to

If you want the best quality in fruits and vegetables, you should buy them loose so that you can pick the nicest pieces yourself. Loose produce is also usually fresher—but it costs more than prepackaged goods.

marinate strips of carrots, cucumbers, string beans, and cauliflower, which can be served as cocktail snacks.

☐ Fresh parsley doesn't stay fresh long—unless you freeze it. Simply snip off what you need without defrosting the whole bunch.

☐ Wilted lettuce can be freshened by letting it stand for 15 minutes or so in cold water with a few drops of lemon juice in it. This doesn't put the lost nutrients back in, though, so don't do it unless you must.

☐ Some chuck roasts contain what is called the "chuck eye". If you can get such a cut, remove this eye from the rest of the meat, and you will have something similar to the more expensive rib eye steak.

☐ February, March, and April are the months in which beef prices are at their lowest.

☐ Large turkeys are meatier than small ones, so you will get more servings per pound if you buy a large bird.

☐ Fillet fish yourself, and you will save about 50 per cent of the cost of ready-to-cook fish.

☐ Raw meat is easier to cut when cold. Meat that has been heated to room temperature becomes mushy and hard to manage. Before you cut it, chill meat in the freezer for about 10 minutes.

☐ Drippings from meat and poultry are great for cooking with, so be sure to save them. Skim off congealed fat from the tops of stews and soups, too. Strain them if necessary, and freeze.

☐ Buying unsliced luncheon meats and slicing them yourself will save about 40 per cent of the cost.

☐ The ingredients listed on packages and cans must, by law, be listed in decreasing order of weight. Thus, a can listing "beef, gravy, ..." will contain more beef (50 per cent minimum) than one listing "gravy, beef ..." The latter may contain only 35 per cent beef.

☐ The top dozen protein buys, according to the U.S. Bureau of Labor Statistics, are: dry beans, peanut butter, whole chicken, canned bean soup, whole milk, eggs, hamburger, beef liver, turkey, canned sardines, canned tuna, and American cheese.

☐ When using whole spices that must be removed from soups and stews before serving, put them in a metal tea ball, and hang the tea ball on the edge of the pot. Seasoning will be right, and removing the spices will be easy.

☐ Buy spices in inexpensive cardboard boxes, and transfer the contents to your regular spice containers—or any small bottles—when you get home.

☐ Stand salad dressing, ketchup, and syrup bottles on their heads to get out the last drops. Liquid will collect in the neck of the bottle, and will pour easily. Be sure to screw the cap on tightly before turning the bottle upside down.

You can afford gourmet dishes by using cheaper cuts of meat—lamb shanks with orange glaze, or beef Stroganoff (with round steak), for example.

☐ Peanut butter will spread more easily and go farther if you add a few drops of hot water to it.

☐ In most recipes requiring olive oil, you can save money by diluting it with a cheaper salad oil. Even when used in a salad dressing, diluted olive oil will hardly be detectable, especially in combination with spices.

☐ When cooking with beer, let it stand for 15 minutes to become still before you use it.

A Pet in the House

Pet ownership brings many rewards and pleasures, and satisfies a person's love for animals. However, you must always remember that you also have responsibilities if you have a pet, and you should think about all the pros and cons before you decide to keep one—or more—of any kind.

Most people like animals, and owning a pet can be fun for young and old. Never overlook the fact, however, that responsibility comes with the fun of pet ownership. When your dog begs for his early morning walk, your cat needs worming, or your parakeet picks up dirty words—remember, you have to take care of your pet whether it's inconvenient or not. The hints in this section will help you be the owner of a happy pet.

☐ It is irresponsible and unkind to let your pet bear litter after litter. Many people hesitate to have their pets altered for fear it will spoil their personality. On the contrary. Alteration often saves females from becoming ill-tempered, restless, and sometimes dangerous. Humane associations all over the country recommend the alteration of pets.

☐ Distemper is one of the most serious diseases your cat or dog can get, so be sure to have the animal inoculated against it at about one year of age. The symptoms of the disease are vomiting, loss of appetite, weakness, diarrhea or constipation, and dehydration, and they appear very suddenly. Isolate the sick animal, do not feed him, keep him warm, and get him to the vet as fast as possible. If your pet should die of distemper, wait at least six months before getting another. Under the right conditions, the distemper virus can live in the atmosphere that long.

☐ If your pet refuses to eat a certain food, don't force him to, unless the vet has prescribed it. If the food has been prescribed, combine it with food your pet likes, and increase the proportion gradually as the animal becomes used to it.

☐ Fresh water should always be made available to both cats and dogs. This is very important if you feed them dry food.

☐ Organ meats are good for cats and dogs, but they can cause diarrhea. If you feed them to your pet, do so in small amounts.

☐ Unless you raise and show dogs for a living, the only advantage in buying an expensive purebred pup is knowing what it will look like when it grows up. The only indication of a mongrel's mature size is the size of its paws—big feet mean the pup will become a big dog.

☐ The size of your home and the amount of time you can spend exercising your dog should determine what breed you buy. Toys and terriers need less exercise than beagles and working breeds, for example, and are usually better off in city apartments.

☐ If you don't want to spend a great deal of time grooming your dog, avoid the long-haired breeds, such as poodles, scotties, Yorkshire terriers, and sheepdogs. Their coats need constant care. Remember, however, that longhaired dogs are better able to tolerate cold climates than short-haired ones.

☐ Your dog can sleep indoors or out most of the year, but once you make your choice, don't change it suddenly. The dog's body will adjust to either the indoor or outdoor temperature, and switching back and forth all the time will disturb his adjustment. This will lower his resistance to infection.

☐ Kennel floors should be at least four inches off the ground. If they are lower, the dampness will make it easy for fleas to breed.

☐ Despite the claims of advertisements, dogs do not like or need variety in their food. Find a good quality commercial food that your dog likes, and stick to it. A steady, unchanging diet will prevent a dog from developing finicky eating habits. Any necessary changes

Above: buying a dog? Keep in mind that a female usually will have a better disposition and be easier to train than a male. Females are also less likely to become attached to one member of the family in preference to all the others.

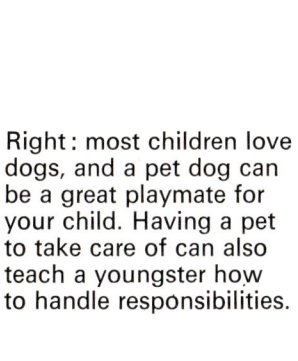

Right: most children love dogs, and a pet dog can be a great playmate for your child. Having a pet to take care of can also teach a youngster how to handle responsibilities.

11

in diet should be gradual to avoid upsetting your dog's stomach. Serve food at room temperature.

☐ Dogs that live indoors like to have a corner with a bed to themselves. Small ones should have a box with a small rug, blanket, or towels in it. Larger dogs need a good-sized mat or thick rug. The bed should be kept clean and out of drafts, but should not be put near a radiator, or the dog's coat will dry out.

☐ Don't give a teething pup brittle bones to chew. They crack easily, and can catch in his throat or stomach. The best type is the knuckle or flat beef bone. Older dogs should chew only rawhide or nylon bones.

☐ Never give your dog toys with bells or other dangles that might be chewed off and swallowed.

☐ When bathing your dog, make a ring of suds around his neck. This will keep fleas from moving up to his head.

☐ Walking a young dog with an older, well-trained one is often a great help in curb training. Dogs tend to be mimics, and the younger one will probably follow the good example of the other.

☐ To give your cat a pill, hold his head in one hand, and gently press his jaws open. Drop the pill in quickly, and push it as far back as you can. Close his mouth and hold it shut, encouraging him to swallow by stroking his throat.

☐ Cats that refuse to eat from a spoon should be given liquid medicines from an eye dropper or squeeze bottle. Slowly release the medicine into the side of the cat's mouth, holding its lips open. Try to keep the cat calm so that it won't move its head about. Cats can swallow only with their mouths closed and heads level.

☐ Feed your cat a teaspoonful of salad oil, or dab vaseline on his nose each week, to prevent hairballs from forming.

☐ Make sure your cat's collar is loose enough for him to pull his head out of, in case the collar gets caught on something. You can buy safety collars that have a strip of elastic.

☐ Scratching is instinctive behavior in cats, and, although you may not like it, you should

A girl and her cat make loving companions. Cats generally need less care than dogs, and like the indoors better, and so may make the perfect pet for apartment dwellers. Remember, though, a cat is not especially good with the very young.

not punish your cat for it. To keep household damage to a minimum, buy your cat a scratching post from a pet supply store. You can also make one yourself by covering a log with carpet, or using a section of a tree trunk with the bark left on. Any scratching board should be fastened upright securely, and should be as tall as your cat is long when he is fully stretched out.

☐ Since cats don't respond to the human voice the way dogs do, you have to rely more on swats and nudges to train them. Hit just hard enough to get your point across.

☐ If you don't want your cat on the furniture, keep pushing him off it until he learns his lesson. Don't expect him to stay out of

rooms if you leave the doors open. Cats always let their curiosity lead them into any accessible place.

☐ Small bones can easily become lodged across the roof of a cat's mouth, and choke him. A cat with something caught in his mouth will claw his jaw, and rub his face on the ground. Wrap his legs and body in a towel, pry his jaws open with your fingers, and pull his head back. Use a spoon handle, curved side up, to dislodge the bone. If it is well down in his throat, use tweezers instead. If you can't reach it easily, give up and rush him to the vet.

☐ Pregnant cats should begin receiving larger meals from the fourth week of pregnancy on. (The gestation period is about 63 days.) A daily dose of vitamin D, calcium, and a little olive oil will also benefit the cat. A few weeks before the kittens are due, put a newspaper lined box in a dim corner or closet, and let the mother begin sleeping there.

Is there something in the way your cat behaves that makes you think it is ill? Does it have definite symptoms, such as vomiting or runny eyes? Get it to the vet right away! A sick cat's condition worsens rapidly, and speedy care is needed.

☐ Always have "Unidote" on hand. This universal antidote can be used if your cat shows symptoms of poisoning—vomiting, diarrhea, drooling, weakness, convulsions, fever, bloody urine. Use the antidote, and then get to the vet immediately.

☐ Don't feed your kitten solid food and milk at the same time. This can cause diarrhea.

☐ Neuter male kittens at about the age of five months, and spay females at 11 weeks. Neither operation is dangerous. Either can be done at a later date, but if you delay spaying a female, you may have a litter of kittens on your hands. Spayed and neutered

Above: if you like your budgerigar to fly loose in the house, make sure that all doors and windows are screened or shut. Otherwise, your pet bird may fly away.

Right: guinea pigs are usually easily contented, and seldom try to wander off, so you can let yours roam around the room for exercise without any fear of losing it. If you take it outdoors, keep a careful watch that it is not attacked by a cat; it may be taken for a rat.

cats have a tendency to gain weight, so watch their diet.

☐ Don't expect your cat to enjoy being walked on a leash. Although you may be able to get her out on a leash, don't think for one moment she will take to it like a dog does. If you insist on a leash, use a harness instead of a collar. This will prevent the cat from slipping off the leash and running away if she should panic.

☐ If your housebroken cat suddenly seems to have a lapse, don't punish it. Cats are clean animals, and usually have good reason for not controlling themselves. Possible causes are illness, loneliness, or the presence of people or other animals she is afraid of.

☐ Commercial repellents are useful in housebreaking your cat. Once she has learned her lesson, you can stop using repellent—but keep some on hand to use for other training purposes, such as keeping her off the new chair or rug. Moth balls can be used in place of commercial repellents. Rub flakes of moth balls into the furniture or furnishings your cat seems to like. Use only a small amount however; cats have a highly developed sense of smell.

☐ Canaries don't need as many playthings as parakeets do. Supply yours with a cuttlebone, perches, and food and water cups. Spread bird gravel over the floor covering, which should be removable for easy cleaning, and put a dish filled with water at room temperature inside the cage for a bath.

☐ Keep all birds out of drafts. If you notice any symptoms of illness, call the vet immediately. The most important factor in caring for a sick bird is speed.

You should always use both hands to pick up a rabbit—one holding the hindquarters, and one grasping the scruff of the neck. Never pick it up by the ears.

☐ When you buy a canary, get a written guarantee that it is a male, and that it will sing within two weeks. Females don't sing. Males sometimes remain silent if they do not take to their new home, or become ill.

☐ Don't be fooled by what appears to be a full food cup in a bird's cage. Empty seed hulls can collect there and give the appearance of being uneaten food. So check regularly to see whether a refill is in order. Your bird will die after 24 hours without food or water.

☐ To teach your parakeet to talk, isolate him from other birds for the first week or two. Let him get used to his new home, and your voice. Don't have more than one person do the teaching. Keep repeating an easy word until he says it. This may take a while, but be patient. Lessons should be about 15 minutes long, twice a day. Don't try for a longer lesson because parakeets bore easily. After the first word, the rest will be easier.

☐ Hamsters need warmth—about 70 degrees—and protection from drafts. If the temperature is too low they will go into hibernation. Hamsters can catch colds from human beings, so they should be kept isolated if any members of your family are ill.

☐ Since hamsters are nearsighted, they often mistake a finger poked into their cage for the end of a carrot. Remind your children of this from time to time.

☐ Stale food should be cleaned out of a hamster's cage every day. However, hamsters have a natural tendency to hoard food, and shouldn't be left without any scraps. Leave him some dry food that won't spoil—raisins or sunflower seeds—to hoard in the cage.

☐ Hamsters and guinea pigs are inclined to tip over water dishes left in their cage. Give them a gravity flow water bottle instead; they won't be able to upset it.

☐ Hamsters are nocturnal animals, so remember that waking them during their daytime sleep is liable to result in a nip.

☐ Male and female hamsters often fight with

each other when they are put in the same cage to breed. Be on hand to separate them if they should fight. Remember also that hamsters reproduce at an alarmingly rapid rate, and shouldn't be bred so often that you have a population explosion on your hands.

☐ Cover the top of an aquarium with wire mesh; spread cedar shavings, shredded newspaper, or kitty litter on the floor; add an exercise wheel and a couple of ladders, and you've got an excellent home for your gerbil or mouse.

☐ Your mouse cage will need a weekly cleaning with disinfectant to get rid of odors. Gerbils are not as odorous as mice, because they don't urinate a great deal. Clean the gerbil's cage thoroughly every two weeks.

☐ Your mouse will enjoy having a hard piece

of wood to chew on to keep its teeth healthy.

☐ Keep gerbils in separate cages unless you want to breed them. They choose one mate only, and they may not accept another if that one dies. Several mice can be caged together, but be careful that they are of the same sex, or you will have more mice than you can handle.

☐ Gerbils and mice are good jumpers, so let them jump out of your hands onto a table top. However, pad the table with a towel so the animals won't get hurt.

☐ Rabbits make gentle pets once they get used to human contact. Those kept indoors should have all-wire cages. Outdoor hutches can be made of wood, with a wire mesh door and floor. Rabbit hutches should be three or more feet off the ground to avoid dampness, and the roof should provide good protection against rain. Any cage should have a pullout tray bottom of metal to make cleaning easier.

☐ Rabbit pellets should be the staple of your pet's diet, but some fresh vegetables daily are good for it. Sprinkle salt on carrots, lettuce, sweet potatoes, or beets for your rabbit. As a special treat, give it wholewheat bread soaked in milk. Remove leftovers within half an hour of feeding.

☐ When breeding your rabbit, put the female into the male's cage, not vice versa. She may not like having him in her cage. Rabbits should not breed until they are at least eight months old.

☐ Artificial plants are best for your fish tank. Growing plants underwater is an art in itself, and live plants make it harder to keep the tank clean. Keep settings natural—that is, be careful not to use marine materials in a freshwater tank.

☐ Beginners should buy an assortment of inexpensive fish, such as barbs, guppies, platys, tetras, and small angels, to start with. It's better to gain experience before trying more expensive species.

☐ Buy the biggest tank you have room for and can afford. A smaller tank is not much cheaper, and is harder to keep clean. Also, the equipment for larger tanks is more efficient. Aim for a tank of more than 10 gallons, and you'll have a good aquarium.

☐ Aquarium sand is sold in pet shops. Before you put sand in the tank, be sure to wash it under running water. When the water runs clear, the sand is ready to go into the tank.

☐ You are more apt to kill your pet fish by overfeeding than by any other mistake in care. Feed only once a day, and sprinkle in only the amount of food that it can consume in 10 minutes. You can leave fish unfed for a week without great harm.

☐ Keep your pet turtle warm at from 75° to 85°F. Turtles are extremely cold-blooded, and, therefore, unable to maintain their

Use one gallon of water to one inch of fish in your aquarium. Also make sure there is enough air space at the top—50 square inches to each fish you have.

proper body temperature at a constant level.
☐ Turtles need vitamin D to keep their shells hard, and they get it from exposure to sun. Glass blocks vitamin D rays, so, whenever it's warm enough, take your turtle out of his terrarium and put him in the backyard for a good sunning. If you are an apartment dweller, a window box makes a good solarium.
☐ Turtles have strange eating habits, and this often makes them victims of malnutrition. They may be happy to eat just about the same things that you do, or may switch from vegetarian to carnivorous overnight, and then back again the next day. Try chicken, fish, raw meat, fruits and vegetables, and cheese. Your turtle should like something from the group.
☐ If your chameleon's color looks bad, he may not be warm enough. Let him rest in the palm of your hand, or in the sun, until he seems happy again. Placing a light bulb near his terrarium is a good way to make sure that he gets enough warmth when it's cloudy or cold. Don't put the bulb too near, however.
☐ Spray your chameleon's terrarium a few times a day. This will keep your pet moist, and also give it dew to drink off the leaves.
☐ A piece of raw fruit placed inside a terrarium will attract the insects your chameleon loves to eat. Your pet shop can sell you whatever the chameleon needs when flying insects become scarce in the colder months of the year.

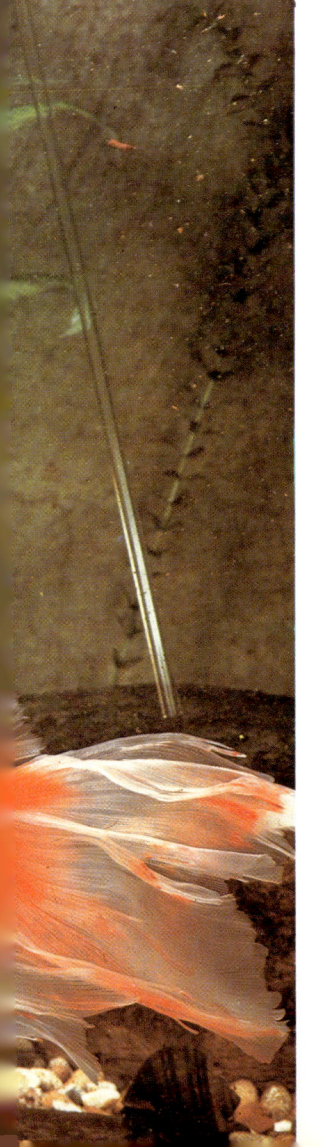

That gentle and affectionate raccoon will probably get nastily ill-tempered when it grows up. At that time, it should be set free near its original home.

Furniture Fix-ups

Are all your kitchen chairs suffering from a case of loose rung disease? Is the desk drawer that sticks driving you mad? Do you feel like crying over the burn you found on your favorite walnut table after your last party? All these matters of furniture care are easily handled if you know a few little tricks—and this section will help give you the know-how you need. Fixing chairs, unsticking drawers, and removing scratches, stains, and burns from wood and all kinds of laminates are among the useful tips you'll find.

☐ Wooden chair rungs tend to become loose, especially in winter when humidity is lower. To tighten a rung that's very loose, pull it out of the socket. Scrape the old glue from both the rung and socket, and give each a coating of white glue; replace the rung in the socket immediately. Make a cord tourniquet to hold the rung in place firmly: tie a piece of cord around the chair to pull the parts together, place wood blocks under the rope where it might rub, and slip a stick through the rope, turn it, and wind it until the freshly glued parts are pulled firmly together. Clean off excess glue.

☐ Chair rungs that are only slightly loose can be tightened simply by injecting adhesive in the gap around the rung. Injected adhesive will swell the wood. Tip the chair on its side so that the adhesive is injected downward.

☐ String is used to repair chair rungs around which there is a gap of $\frac{1}{8}$ inch or more. Remove the old glue from the rung end, and give it a new coating. Wrap string over the glue snugly. Apply glue to the inside of the socket, and insert the rung. Secure with a tourniquet, and cut off any excess string with a single edged razor.

☐ Wood swells when humidity increases, and drawers tend to stick. Use paraffin, candle wax, or a silicon spray on the spot where the drawer sticks.

☐ If lubrication fails to make a drawer pull smoothly, you must sand it at the points where it sticks. Before sanding, remove the lubrication with detergent or turpentine.

☐ A drawer will sometimes become stuck so tightly that you can't pull it out far enough to reach the part that needs lubricating. In such cases, you must dry the wood by placing a droplight (a bulb protected by a wire cage) inside the drawer, or by aiming a warm air flow into the drawer from a hair dryer. If you

The chair that is junk to someone else may be exactly what you want for your kitchen or den. It's fun to get a bargain in a junk shop, and to paint your purchase yourself. It's also a money saver.

can't budge the drawer at all, the droplight or hair dryer can be put in the one just above or below it.

☐ One corner of a drawer sometimes pushes in too far. In this case, cut a block of wood, and glue it in the back corner. This will keep the drawer from going in too far. Cut the wood to the same height as the back of the drawer. Measure how much too far the drawer goes in, and make the block of wood that same thickness.

☐ When using clamps to hold glued joints, place wooden blocks under the clamp where it meets the wood. This will prevent damage to the wood surface. Wax paper should be placed between the block and the wood surface to keep the block from becoming stuck down with excess glue.

☐ Superficial scratches in wood can be camouflaged by any of the following: paste floor wax; nut meats (for walnut and fruitwoods); a mixture of boiled linseed oil, turpentine, and water in equal parts; iodine (for maple and mahogany); or, as a last resort, a matching shade of shoe polish.

☐ Deeper scratches in wood surfaces can be repaired with special wax sticks that resemble children's crayons. Buy a set of these sticks at the hardware store, and select the one that matches the color of the wood best. Rub it

into the scratch; it will cover beautifully.
☐ To repair burns in a wooden surface, first scrape the burned portion clean with a sharp knife, following the grain of the wood. Wipe the area with benzine, then rub gently with fine sandpaper or steel wool. Refinish with a matching shade of oil stain. If burns are deep, use stick shellac instead of oil stain.
☐ Water and alcohol stains on wood can sometimes be removed with a paste of castor oil and cigarette ashes. If this doesn't work, apply some spirits of camphor to the stain with a clean rag, and allow it to dry for 45 minutes. Put some machine oil on a cloth, dip the cloth in rottenstone, and rub the stain in the direction of the grain. Finally, rub the damaged area with paste wax or, if necessary, refinish.
☐ Stains may be removed from marble with a paste of hydrogen peroxide and powdered whiting. Apply paste to stain, and add a sprinkling of ammonia. Place plastic wrap over paste to keep it from drying out. Let stand a few minutes, and rinse with hot water.
☐ Rub heat marks in wood with spirits of camphor, then with a soft, dry cloth. If this doesn't work, treat as for water and alcohol stains.
☐ Before repairing loose veneers, place a damp cloth over the damaged area, and lay a warm iron on the cloth. The veneer will become more pliable because of increased moisture, and will, therefore, be less apt to break when lifted.
☐ Gently pull loose veneer away from furniture, being careful not to break it. Clean out any old glue. Apply fresh glue, press veneer down, and secure with a clamp, masking tape, or a weight, depending upon where the repair has been made. Clean off any excess glue, and let dry.
☐ To repair veneer when a section has broken off, first use a fresh single edged blade to cut out a square or rectangle around the damaged area. Remove old glue. On a carefully matched sheet of veneer, cut out a patch to fit the space exactly. Glue patch in place, and secure with a clamp, masking tape, or a weight. Refinish to match.

Do you want to glue a cup handle on, or stick a piece of wood veneer back in place on a table? Knowing the best cement to use with various materials can save you a lot of trouble, and this chart gives you an easy reference to what sticks what.

☐ To repair loose plastic laminate, lift up the loose section gently, and apply a generous amount of contact cement with a cheap paintbrush. Spread the cement over the two surfaces by pressing the laminate down, but quickly raise it up again. Use a fork to keep the two surfaces apart for about an hour, while the cement dries. Remove the fork, and bond the laminate to the surface with a few good whacks with your fist.
☐ *ABS* is a strong heat molded material that won't dent or chip, but may scratch. Rub toothpaste on surface scratches with a damp cloth. Use a mild dishwashing detergent for everyday care.
☐ *Laminate plastics* are made of filler materials, often paper, and resins bonded into single sheets with heat and pressure. An example of this is Formica. It is used for table and counter tops, cabinets, etc. Laminates are strong, and resist heat up to 275°F. Never place dishes hot from the oven on the surface, however. To remove stains, use nothing stronger than Lava soap. For daily care, wipe with a damp sponge.
☐ *Acrylic sheet plastic* is light, strong, and can be clear, opaque, tinted, or colored. Clean with cotton flannel dipped in a solution of gentle dishwashing detergent and water. Never use strong detergents or solvents. Car wax of good quality may be used to wax acrylic sheet plastic, which will remove small surface scratches. To remove deeper scratches, sand gently with 400 grit sandpaper, and buff with a muslin wheel and fine grit buffing compound.
☐ *Fiberglass* is composed of glass fiber reinforced plastic, molded into shape. It is extremely strong and light. For ordinary care, use Lestoil and warm water. Mild powdered detergents rubbed on with a sponge are best for stains. Don't use anything harsh. Wax with car wax or clear liquid wax.

What Sticks What?

MATERIALS	Mucilage	Animal Glue	Resin Glue	Polyvinyl Resin Glue	Casein Glue	Rubber Cement	Epoxy Cement	Contact Cement	Steel Paste	Rubber Sealant	Resorcinol Glue	Liquid Vinyl Cement	Aluminum Cement	Polystyrene Cement
Wood to Wood and Plywood		●	●	●	●						●			
Plywood Wall Panels			●					●						
Plastic Laminates, Wood to Wood			●	●	●			●			●			
Hardboard to Wood		●	●	●				●			●			
Wood Veneering		●	●	●										
Wood—Outdoors											●			
Wood Boats											●			
Styrene Plastic to Styrene Plastic														●
Metal to Wood							●	●						
China		●		●			●		●	●		●	●	●
Patch, Seal and Solder							●		●				●	
Caulk										●				
Model Building, Felt to Wood		●		●								●		●
Leather to Leather or Wood	●	●				●		●				●		
Unlike Materials							●	●						
Paper to Paper or Fabrics	●	●		●		●						●		
Canvas to Wood		●		●		●		●						
Rubber to Wood or Metal						●		●						
Metal to Metal							●		●					
Leather to Paper	●													
Leaks in Pipes and Steel										●				

Remove that Stain

You don't have to rush to the cleaner's with every annoying stain on your clothes. Try some of these tips to take quick and effective action yourself.

Alcoholic beverages — Soak in cold water before stain has a chance to set; then sponge with liquid detergent, and rinse, putting a few drops of vinegar in rinse water. Launder.

Blood — Soak in cold water, then wash with detergent in warm water. If stain persists, soak in lukewarm water, to which ammonia has been added in the proportion of three tablespoons of ammonia to a gallon of water, for at least half an hour; wash with detergent again.

Chewing gum — Apply an ice cube to harden gum, then scrape off as much as possible with a dull knife. Sponge affected area with cleaning fluid, repeating applications as necessary. If a sugar stain remains, sponge with water.

Chocolate — Treat stain with cool water and detergent. Rinse spot thoroughly and let dry, then sponge remaining greasy portion with cleaning fluid. A bleach is sometimes necessary to remove all traces of the stain.

Coffee and Tea — Soak in cool water. If either beverage contained milk, apply cleaning fluid to garment, soak in cold water, and wash in warm suds.

Cosmetics

Sponge with heavy detergent suds. Repeat until all signs of the stain has gone. On some fabrics, letting the material dry between applications of detergent may produce better results. If cosmetics are greasy, follow directions for removing grease stains.

Egg

Be careful never to use hot water, or stain may become permanently set. If stain has dried, scrape off as much as possible, then sponge with cold water. Work detergent into stain; then launder as usual, using bleach if recommended. Fabrics with special finishes may need further treatment with a spray stain remover for washable fabrics (see Grease).

Fruits and Berries

Always sponge fresh stains promptly with cool water before they have time to set. Some stains, such as those from citrus fruits, are invisible when dry, and turn yellow with age or in the presence of heat. In that state they are difficult to remove. Where boiling water can be used, stretch stained portion of fabric over a bowl, and pour boiling water through it. If stain remains, sponge with lemon juice solution or hydrogen peroxide. Where boiling water cannot be used, sponge stain well with cool water. Work glycerin into spot, and let stand for several hours. Then add a few drops of white vinegar, rinse thoroughly, and launder.

Grass and Flowers

Sponging with rubbing alcohol will remove most plant stains from washable and non-washable fabrics. Dilute with two parts water for acetate, and always pretest colors to see if they are affected. Or, work liquid detergent into the stain, and rinse. Launder, using a bleach safe for that particular fabric.

Grease

Scrape off as much as possible, sponge with liquid detergent, then launder as usual. Noniron fabrics may also be treated with a solution of two tablespoons of washing soda to a cup of warm water. Rub it into dampened spot, and allow to remain for not more than five minutes. If stain persists after either method, sponge with cleaning fluid, let dry, and repeat until stain is gone. Another method is to use one of the new spray stain removers. Spray it on stain, and launder according to directions on package.

Ice cream and Milk

Sponge or soak in cold water. Rub detergent into the spot, and launder. Remove any grease with cleaning fluid. If stain persists, bleach according to fibre.

Ink, ballpoint

Ordinary laundering (with bleach, if recommended) will wash out some types of ballpoint ink; others need special treatment, and may be set by washing. To determine which type the stain is, mark a similar piece of fabric with the same ink, and wash. If laundering does not remove mark, pour denatured alcohol through fabric (testing first on scrap), or rub white petroleum jelly into stain, soak in detergent solution, and launder. You can also spray with hair spray until soaking wet, then scrub by hand, using a thick solution of liquid detergent. (If fabric is not likely to be harmed by a small amount of abrasion, rubbing the stain with an eraser especially designed to remove ballpoint ink before you try any of these other methods may do the trick.)

Ink, regular — Run cold water through stain until it runs clear, then rub in thick detergent suds. Let stand, then launder, using bleach, if recommended. If stain persists, sponge with chlorine bleach or hydrogen peroxide and baking soda on stain, and steam. However, all of these methods may effect the color. You might also try a solution of one part of alcohol to two parts of water, then full-strength alcohol. Some ink is permanent, and can't be removed.

Ketchup — Scrape off excess. Sponge stain promptly with cool water. Or, soak fabric in cold water for 30 minutes or more. Some stains may need to be soaked overnight. After sponging or soaking, work liquid detergent or a detergent paste (dry detergent mixed with a small amount of water) into the stain, and rinse. If stain remains, you will have to use a bleach.

Mildew — Rub off as much as possible, then wash in warm, soapy water, and rinse.

Mud — Let dry, then rub with a stiff brush. Sponge in cool water, then launder in hot water. If stain remains, sponge with rubbing alcohol.

Mustard — With washable fabrics, apply liquid detergent to dampened stain, and rinse. If stain is stubborn, place article in hot detergent solution, and let stand for several hours or overnight. If results are still not satisfactory, use bleach. Mustard stains are almost impossible to remove from plastic materials.

Paint — Stains must be treated before they're dry, or they will be almost impossible to remove. If they're from an oil-based paint, sponge with turpentine (testing fabric first), then launder, using bleach, if recommended. If stains are from a water-based paint, sponge with liquid detergent, and launder.

Perspiration — Always wash or sponge off immediately with warm water containing detergent. If colors have been affected, sponge fresh stain with ammonia, an old stain with vinegar. Rinse carefully with water. If oily traces remain when fabric is dried, sponge with cleaning fluid. Yellow stains that remain after the detergent treatment may require use of bleach.

Rust — Rub lemon juice into stained area, and, before it dries, rinse in warm water.

Soft drinks — Sponge immediately with cool water, then launder. Some soft drink stains are invisible after they dry, but turn yellow with age or exposure to heat. This yellow stain is impossible to remove.

Shoe polish — Scrape off as much as possible, and rub gently with dry cleaning fluid. Once the cleaning rag is soiled, turn to a new side.

Wine — Apply salt and club soda to stained area to absorb the wine. Sponge with cold water.

Entertainingly Yours

Entertaining is one of the things that makes life fun. Whether it's a party you've planned weeks ahead, or an impromptu get-together on the spur of the moment, entertaining is the easiest road to making and keeping friends. Of course, it's important that your style of entertaining be appropriate to your whole lifestyle—and if you keep your entertaining to scale, you should always be able to have as much enjoyment out of it as your guests. It's the too ambitious or too elaborate party that can put a hostess and host into a panic. In the following pages are many welcome tips on ways to cut down on the work before, during, and after a party, as well as some delightful ideas on novel kinds of parties. Maybe one of these ideas will be just right for the social you're giving in two weeks; others might spare you some of the nervousness you get before the doorbell announces the arrival of the first guest. All are meant to help you be a more relaxed, more successful hostess.

☐ The disadvantage of party invitations given by telephone is that they often don't give reluctant guests time to think of how to refuse graciously. To avoid this, tell prospective guests when and what kind of party it is *before* you ask whether they can come.

☐ Make invitations clear. No one likes to be caught without a present because they didn't know it was a birthday party, or come dressed in blue jeans when others are wearing dressier clothes, or starve because your invitation led guests to believe you were serving dinner. Place, date, time, length, kind of party, and suggestions for dress are all facts that should be on an invitation.

☐ Keep an accurate, up-to-date file of the names and addresses of your friends. If you should decide on a spur-of-the-moment party, you will have no trouble with your guest list—or your nerves.

☐ Planning ahead will save you time and energy on the day of your party, and can also save money. It will give you time to shop around for the best food buys, especially delicacies. If your supermarket offers gourmet specialties on sale, stock up ahead of time.

☐ In writing down your party plans, make two lists: one of items you can buy ahead of time, the other of those you must buy the day before or the day of the party.

☐ If a guest brings you a bottle of wine as a gift, you may put it away and save it for some future evening if you want to. It is not necessary to serve it that same night.

☐ Inviting too many guests for the size of your home won't add to anyone's enjoyment. A good way to have a lot of guests, but still stay within bounds, is to invite your guests in shifts—half of them for the first two hours, and the remainder for the following two hours.

☐ If you have an impulse to serve an exotic menu, save it for small, intimate parties with guests whose tastes you know. It may seem dull to have creamed chicken, but it's pretty sure to satisfy most people at a large party. Dishes you don't feel confident about preparing don't belong at your party.

☐ Consider any dietary restrictions your guests may have because of health or religion. Don't go overboard, but if you suspect any are on a special diet, simply ask. They will appreciate your thoughtfulness.

☐ Some of your guests may find it hard to bear cigarette and cigar smoke. A brandy snifter half filled with white vinegar, and with a flower floating on top, will help. It is not only considerate, but also attractive.

☐ Should you be giving a birthday party without knowing the age of the guest of honor, place the candles on the cake in the form of a question mark. It will usually make a hit with everyone.

the groupings of seats in your living room will allow. Otherwise, someone will be left standing, which will make him feel left out.

☐ Your guests may offer to help you serve or clean up. If you need help, accept the offer, but not without giving your volunteer clear, explicit instructions. Helter-skelter races to and from the kitchen will spoil the relaxed atmosphere.

☐ Unless you prepare ahead of time, week-

Left: planning ahead is a big key to successful entertaining. It helps to make two lists: one of things you can buy in advance, and one of things you must get the day before, or of, the party.

Right: if you've planned well for a party, you'll be able to relax and enjoy it as much as your guests when it's held.

☐ Juggling a plate while trying to help oneself at a buffet dinner can take some of the fun out of the meal. If you leave space between serving platters on the table, guests can set down their plates while serving themselves. To be sure no guests have a long wait for food, set up two identical buffet tables.

☐ If relaxed conversation is the highlight of your parties, don't invite more guests than

end guests can keep you slaving in the kitchen the whole time. Clean and cut up vegetables in advance, prepare casseroles to be popped in the oven, and, for breakfast, simply leave eggs, bread and butter, bacon, and coffee near the stove so your guests can help themselves in a leisurely manner at their own time.

☐ The greatest pitfall for the hostess with weekend guests is overplanning. Remember, your guests need some time for just sitting and relaxing—perhaps alone—so don't plan too many activities.

☐ If you are going to serve an elaborate main course, save time and energy by keeping the dessert simple. The one most recommended by gourmets is fresh fruit. Fruit ripened to perfection is a masterpiece in itself. Raw fruit combinations, such as melon balls, strawberries, and blueberries, are easy to do, and delicious. Or try some cheese and crackers.

☐ Even if you are having a relatively formal sit-down dinner, you can take a few shortcuts. Combine your first course with the cocktails, for example. You can have a bowl of shrimp on ice with a sauce dip, various cheeses and crackers, crunchy raw vegetables with dips, or, perhaps, meatballs on toothpicks. A serving cart is invaluable in clearing the table of one course, and bringing in another. When you wheel in the dessert, serve it from the cart, and pass the plates to guests.

☐ It makes a nice change to have your after-dinner coffee in the living room, if you have a separate dining room, of course. This also means you can leave the table uncleared, and just close the door on it till later.

☐ If you are planning two parties during the Christmas season, consider giving them on consecutive nights. You will have to do only one major housecleaning, make one big shopping trip, and decorate once. It can also be cheaper if you plan the food for both nights together. For example, you might have a roast turkey the first night, and a cold buffet, including turkey leftovers, the second.

☐ Asking one of your guests to assist you can have definite advantages if you go about it the right way. It will make a guest feel truly part of the party, give a newcomer a chance to circulate widely, and provide singles with an opportunity to initiate conversations with other singles.

☐ Introducing a guest to six or seven other people at the same time is not a good idea. Not only does the person being introduced feel all eyes on her, but also she will find it almost impossible to remember so many names. Don't introduce anyone to more than two or three people at a time.

☐ Don't make the mistake of thinking hospitality consists of forcing food on your guests. Offering seconds is fine, but don't constantly urge your guests to sample this or that specialty, or to have just one more drink.

☐ Emptying ash trays and removing dirty glasses are the only cleaning chores a hostess should do during the party. Do them quietly,

27

and resist impulses to wipe the coffee table, and plump the pillows, or you will make your guests uncomfortable. Remember that ash trays in every nook and cranny are your best protection against cigarette burns, scattered ashes, and unwanted stubs in the coffee cups.

☐ During the dinner, try to talk with the person on either side of you in turn, so as to neglect neither. If your table is small, of course, conversation that includes everyone will occur naturally.

☐ Easy, fast, and convenient—that's a garage party. Staple old quilts or bright swatches of fabric to the walls, cover bare bulbs with wicker basket shades, and set up folding tables covered with felt and potted plants, and you're all set. Best of all, when the party's over, you can just close the door, return to an uncluttered house, and leave the party debris until morning.

☐ Good idea for a Sunday afternoon—a revolving meal. Get together eight friends, and visit four homes in a leisurely fashion, having a different course at each place. Start with drinks and hors d'oeuvres at the first. Move on to the second for the main course, to the third for salad, fruit, and cheese, and the fourth for dessert and coffee. Each couple gets a chance to play host and hostess, but all divide the work.

☐ Give a recipe party for the bride-to-be. Each of the guests brings her favorite recipe, and writes it into an autograph book at the party. The recipient will have a collection of time-honored and tested recipes, and also something to remember her friends by.

☐ How about an international party that includes your friends from foreign countries? Fly the flags of your guests' homelands for decoration.

☐ Ask each guest you invite to a party to bring someone he or she thinks you would enjoy meeting. It is a good chance to meet new people and make new friends.

☐ Don't knock yourself out cooking for guests who stay longer than a weekend. Plan on at least one dinner of take-out foods—a

Above: it will be easier and less confusing for your guest if you introduce her to only two or three others at one time. Left: a good party idea is to honor friends who are going abroad for a vacation. Do it by serving traditional dishes of the country to which they are going. It will give them a nice preview of what they can expect to be eating. Here the buffet is amply spread with Scandinavian food.

delispread, pizza, or Chinese food.

☐ Have a luncheon or supper to which each guest contributes a dish. Keep plenty of plastic wrap and containers on hand so that contributors can take leftovers home. Also, prepare labels in advance to put on each guests' dishes so these will not be lost or mixed up.

☐ Give a morning coffee party with many variants of coffee. Serve American and expresso coffee with a choice of whipped cream, lemon and orange twists, liqueurs, brandy, hot chocolate, cinnamon, nutmeg, chocolate shavings, or cream. Guests can experiment on their own, or work from recipes you supply. A light buffet is also called for.

☐ Collect all avid chess, bridge, or monopoly players you know and have a game party. Have a tournament, and finish with a championship playoff.

☐ Try an apéritif buffet instead of a cocktail party. Not only are apéritifs less expensive, but they are also easier to serve, most of them requiring no mixers. There is a wide variety available, among them sherry, vermouth champagne, Campari, Dubonnet, Lillet, and San Raphael. Some people enjoy a Madeira or port as a predinner drink, although they are most often taken after dinner.

☐ Give a "half-and-half" party to enlarge your circle of acquaintances. Throw the party in honor of a friend, who invites half the guests. You invite the other half. You can do the same thing by co-hostessing a party, and splitting the guest list between you.

☐ Have a hobby you're proud of? Make it the point of your party. It's a chance to show off a bottle collection, antiquarian books, or needlework, for example. Label each item like museums do. You'll be surprised how interested your guests will get.

☐ Give a party in honor of friends about to embark on an extended or special vacation. Set up a table decorated with ornaments and pictures of each of the countries they plan to visit. On the buffet, have one traditional dish of each of the countries. Your guests of honor will get a delightful preview of some national dishes, and, in researching the foods and traditions of different countries, you will have an enjoyable learning experience yourself.

☐ Next Christmas season, borrow a happy custom from Finland, and have a *pikkujoulu*. It's a pre-Christmas social at which there's a stand-up meal, music, and dancing. Each guest brings a small gift suitable for anyone, and all the guests draw for a gift in the course of the party. The traditional decoration consists of small trees trimmed in various ways that suit your fancy.

The Table Beautiful

Below: a table that is tastefully set can put everyone into a gala party mood. Settings don't have to be elaborate; attractive arrangement is the key.

A table that looks attractive even before the food is on it somehow perks up the appetite. You don't have to have expensive silver, crystal, and china to set a pretty table, either. Careful choice of colors in the tablecloth and napkins, correctly placed settings, and an interesting centerpiece make all the difference. This section is full of suggestions for little things you can do to brighten and cheer your dinner table. Special attention is given to centerpieces that are easy, inexpensive, and eye-catching.

☐ Making your own tablecloth? You can avoid having a seam down the center. Buy two lengths of fabric, split one in half lengthwise, and sew each half to the ends of the whole piece so that the seams fall at, or near, the edges of the table. By this method you can also do a cloth with contrasting color for the center or end pieces, or a print-with-plain combination.

☐ Bandanas sewn together make a cheap, colorful tablecloth. Use contrasting colors in a checkerboard pattern for even greater interest.

☐ For a look of opulence, spread your dining table with a velvet cloth. These days you can buy velvet that is machine washable, so this is not as impractical as it may sound.

☐ Permanent press sheets come in so many beautiful designs now that they ought to be shown—and they can be if used as tablecloths and napkins.

☐ For Christmas parties, edge red place mats with a fringe of snowflakes embroidered with white angora yarn.

☐ Oilcloth and vinyl make good place mats—and without hemming. Cut them out with pinking shears, and iron appliqués on.

Make or buy the appliqués in the shape of fruits or vegetables in bright colors. Leave one side of the appliqué open so you can insert a napkin.

☐ When serving finger foods, such as corn on the cob or artichokes, tuck a paper napkin inside the cloth one to minimize food stains on the latter. It will also help reduce lipstick stains on the cloth napkins that have to be washed.

Above: checked runners going lengthwise make a long narrow table look bright and cheerful.

☐ You needn't use only candlesticks that match. A group of different heights, shapes, and materials is often effective. Try silver and brass, or silver and glass. If you have a lot of small candle holders, put one at each place setting.

☐ In general, a centerpiece should echo the shape of the table it's on: rectangular, square, or round. However, a centerpiece doesn't always have to be in the center. Try a round one as a replacement for one of the settings on a round table, or use arrangements in pairs directly or diagonally opposite each other on a square table.

☐ Remember that all centerpieces should be low enough for guests to see over easily. Save taller, more dramatic ones for buffet tables, where guests will not be seated.

☐ For greenery and flowers on the table, use ceramic bowls, brass or copper kettles, buckets, baskets, tiered epergnes, and compotes in silver, brass, porcelain, or crystal. The same kind of containers can be used for dried flowers, too. A birdcage painted and filled with flowers and ivy is both attractive and different as a centerpiece. You can sometimes find old, ornate birdcages in a junk shop, or at rummage sales.

☐ When you don't have a centerpiece, use colorful napkins folded and placed in goblets at each place setting, or mass them in the center of the table in vases or glasses.

☐ A colorful centerpiece for a holiday table can be made with empty boxes all prettily gift wrapped.

☐ For an unusual centerpiece, fill clear glass containers with water, colored or plain, and float flowers on the top.

Left: if you want to do a complicated or tall centerpiece, it's best to use it on the buffet table where it will not be in the way of seated guests.

Right: individual trays all set with their own flower, candle, and tableware makes it easy for guests to serve themselves at the buffet, and then eat on their laps.

33

Right: fruit often makes as interesting a centerpiece as flowers—and it's also edible later. This one of beribboned yellow lemons is bright and gay.

Above: take time to beautify the table when you're having your leisurely Sunday breakfast. It will truly add to your enjoyment of the food—and the day off.

☐ You may want to avoid the expense of buying fresh flowers for your party table without giving up the idea of something green and pretty. You can use plants you already have around the house. Put them in decorated pots, or cover the plain pots with foil or crepe paper. Another idea is to buy greens, such as ferns, lemon leaves, or eucalyptus. They are usually reasonable in price, and last much longer than cut flowers. Artificial flowers are expensive, but may appeal to you because of their durability and ease of care. Over a long period, they would be cheaper than fresh flowers.

☐ Make an attractive centerpiece of clippings from your plants, and let each guest who wants one take it home. Long after the party is over, your guests will have a new plant to remember it by.

☐ Spray dried flower arrangements with hair spray. It will keep fluff from plants such as milkweed from falling out.

☐ Potted flowering plants are always lovely on a table. On an informal table, the pots can show if they are well scrubbed. Try three geraniums alternating with candlesticks in a row down the center.

☐ A centerpiece can be made with fruits as well as flowers—and has the additional advantage of being edible. A simple plan is to lay a circle of green felt, covered with smaller circles of white linen, in the center of the table, and place on it a bowl of limes and lemons. Vary the colors of the felt and linen according to the fruits you use. The effect is simple but striking.

☐ Having a lobster meal out of doors? Your main course may be spectacular enough to serve as a centerpiece in itself. A row of whole lobsters just off the fire is a marvelous sight. Remember, too, you need lots of room when you eat lobster, so you won't want a clutter of complicated table decorations.

☐ When choosing flowers for arrangements, don't pick ones that are already in full bloom. They will begin to wilt quickly. If picking flowers from your own garden, do so only in the morning or evening, when it is cool and not too bright.

Drinks and Wine

Sometimes the success of a mixed drink depends on something as simple as using the right kind of ice in it. Find out about this point in the following pages—and use the other useful tips about drinks and wine for your next party.

☐ Prechilling all ingredients will make your drinks as icy as those the professional bartenders make. You can cool the glasses by filling them with crushed ice, and letting them stand while you mix the drinks.

☐ Boil three cups of sugar in one cup of water for several minutes, and chill. This makes a syrup sweetener for drinks. Plain sugar added directly to a drink will form a sediment at the bottom of the glass.

☐ To get more flavor and juice from fresh fruits, soak them in tepid water before you squeeze them into drinks. For the best results, squeeze the fruit just before mixing drinks. Squeezing them even half an hour ahead of time will diminish their flavor.

☐ Drinks containing hard-to-mix ingredients should be shaken hard. Easy-to-blend combinations, on the other hand, should only be stirred. Gentle stirring is in order for drinks containing carbonated beverages.

☐ Shaved ice belongs in drinks that are sipped through straws. Highballs and Old Fashioneds take ice cubes. All other drinks should have cracked ice.

☐ Eggs tend to be congealed by liquor. All ingredients in eggy drinks should, therefore, be blended *before* adding the liquor.

☐ A twist of lemon is often part of a cocktail. To add it properly, rub a narrow strip of peel around the rim of the glass, twist one drip of oil from the peel into the glass, then drop in the peel itself.

☐ A general rule for serving wine: no dry wine after a sweet one, no white after red. Dry wines are served before you eat, and with dinner; sweeter wines go with desserts.

☐ Red wines are usually served with red meat, game, and dishes with strong flavor, while white wines are drunk with more delicate foods, such as chicken and fish.

Left: dining out? Don't be fearful about making a wrong choice of wine. Nowadays it's more a matter of personal taste than of rigid rules, so have what you like best. One tip: a rosé wine always goes with anything.

Right: hot punch is a warming drink for winter, and is easy to do in big quantities for a Christmas party. See the drink chart on page 40 for some good punch recipes.

However, these are no longer hard and fast rules, and you should experiment to find out which wine you prefer with what.

☐ Sparkling red and white wines are served cold. Still white wines and roses are chilled. Still red wines are stored in a cool place, but served at room temperature.

☐ Open still wines one hour prior to serving so that they can "breathe". Sparkling wines are opened just before pouring.

☐ Do champagne descriptions such as "brut", "sec", and "doux" puzzle you? The explanation is simple: these and other adjectives like them refer to the sweetness of the wine. The degree of sweetness not only divides champagne into three types, but also determines what it should be served with. *Brut* champagne is the driest, having no sugar added. You can use it as an apéritif, serve it throughout a meal, and have it as a party drink or at the end of the evening. *Dry*, *sec*, or *extra sec* champagne also goes as an apéritif or with all meat courses, and can be served with nuts and dried fruit. *Sweet*, *doux*, or *demi-sec* champagne is the sweet one. It is served with desserts and pastries.

Mixing Drinks

Martini

All martini drinkers seem to have a favorite—and, to them, sacred—proportion of gin to dry vermouth. What you have to remember in mixing one is that pure gin is not a martini. Four parts gin to one part vermouth is a widely accepted ratio. Remember, too, a chilled glass is an absolute must.

Chill stemmed cocktail glasses in the freezer, the ice cube section, or in crushed ice. Fill the martini pitcher with cracked (not crushed) ice cubes. Use lots of them. Working quickly, pour dry gin and dry vermouth over the ice. Stir quickly about 8 or 10 times, just to get the drink very cold, but without any melted ice in it. Strain at once into the chilled glasses, and twist a thin slice of lemon peel over them. For your guidance, 3 ounces of gin and ¾ ounce vermouth will serve two. Other garnishes can be: pitted olive, cocktail onion, almond-stuffed olive, miniature artichoke heart, or piece of lemon peel. Martini on the rocks is made the same way, but poured over ice cubes into a prechilled Old-Fashioned glass.

If someone at your party asks for a Bloody Mary, are you left floundering at the bar? You won't be if you follow this helpful guide to mixed drinks, which includes several of the most popular ones.

Dry Manhattan

Stir 1½ ounces whiskey, ½ ounce dry (French) vermouth, and 1 dash of orange bitters, with cracked ice. Strain into a chilled 3-ounce stemmed cocktail glass; garnish with a lemon peel.

Sweet Manhattan

Stir 1½ ounces whiskey, ¾ ounce sweet (Italian) vermouth, and 1 dash orange bitters, with cracked ice. Strain into a chilled 3 ounce stemmed cocktail glass; garnish with a maraschino cherry.

Old Fashioned

In a squat heavy-bottomed tumbler, put a lump of sugar, sprinkled with 3 dashes of angostura bitters. Wet this down with 1 teaspoon of water, then dissolve the sugar in the water with a wooden muddler. Add ice, and pour over it 1½ ounces of rye (traditional), or bourbon whiskey. Twist a lemon peel over the top, and stir. You may add a garnish of a maraschino cherry, a slice of orange, or a stick of fresh or canned pineapple. For a variation, try a dash of curaçao.

Daiquiri

Shake with cracked ice until the shaker frosts: the juice of half a lime, 1½ ounces white Bacardi rum, and 1 spoonful of sugar. Strain off into a 3-ounce cocktail glass.

Champagne Cocktail

Rub a lump of sugar along the side of a ripe lemon, scraping off as much lemon zest onto the sugar as possible. Place in a 6-ounce champagne glass with a small lump of ice and a dash of angostura bitters. Slowly fill the glass with chilled champagne, stirring only enough to dissolve the sugar. Serve with a twist of lemon peel.

Toddy

In the bottom of an Old Fashioned glass, crush: ½ teaspoon sugar, 1 teaspoon water, 1 strip of lemon peel about 1 inch long. Add 1 or 2 cubes of ice. Pour in 2 ounces of whiskey, and give a quick stir. Variations: may also be made with 2 ounces of brandy, 2 ounces of gin, or 2 ounces of rum.

Hot Toddy

Put the sugar (½ teaspoon) into a warmed Old Fashioned glass. Add 2 ounces of whiskey (or gin, or rum, or brandy) and 4 ounces of boiling water. Stir, and decorate with a slice of lemon stuck with a clove. Grate a little nutmeg on the top.

Ward Eight

Into a glass half-filled with cracked ice, put 1 teaspoon grenadine, the juice of ½ lemon, 1 teaspoon powdered sugar, and 2 ounces whiskey. Shake briskly, and strain into an 8-ounce stem glass, previously prepared with 2 cubes of ice, slice of orange, lemon, cherry. Variations: add 3 to 4 dashes of orange bitters and 3 dashes of crème de menthe.

Dubonnet Cocktail

Stir well with cracked ice: 1½ ounces Dubonnet, ¾ ounce gin, and a dash of orange bitters. Strain into a 3-ounce cocktail glass, and serve with a twist of lemon peel.

Bloody Mary

Shake with cracked ice, 2 ounces vodka, 2 ounces tomato juice, a dash of lemon juice, pinch of salt, pepper, celery salt, sugar, and ½ teaspoon of Worcestershire sauce. Strain off into an Old Fashioned glass with a cube of ice, or serve on rocks.

Tom Collins

In a shaker, shake well with cracked ice: the juice of ½ a lemon, sugar to taste, and 2 ounces of dry gin. Strain into a 10-ounce glass. Add several ice cubes. Fill with carbonated water, and decorate with lemon, an orange slice, and a cherry. Serve with a straw. May also be made with rye or bourbon, or Holland gin.

Planters' Punch

Put the juice of 2 limes, 2 teaspoons sugar, and 2 ounces of soda water into a 12-ounce glass. Fill it with shaved ice and stir, then add 2 dashes of bitters, and 2½ ounces of rum. Stir and decorate with a cherry, pineapple stick, and orange and lemon slices. Serve with a straw.

Sloe Gin Fizz

Shake well with cracked ice, 2 ounces sloe gin, the juice of ½ a lemon, and 1 teaspoon powdered sugar. Strain off into an 8-ounce glass, fill with soda, and garnish with a lemon slice. Can also be made with rum or dry gin.

Party Punches

For big parties, such as receptions or open house, punches are not only popular and easier to make in quantity, but also go farther for the money. Rum, whiskey, and brandy are the most often used liquors in punches, as these recipes demonstrate.

Champagne Punch

½ cup lemon juice
½ cup water
1 cup sugar
3 ounces brandy
3 ounces curaçao
3 ounces maraschino
1 bottle club soda (large)
3 bottles champagne

In a punch bowl dissolve sugar in water and lemon juice. Add brandy, maraschino, and curaçao. Mix well. Add block of ice. Just before serving pour in chilled club soda and champagne. Stir gently. Garnish with sliced fruits and berries.
Makes 35 four-ounce servings.

Fish House Punch

2 quarts water
1 quart lemon juice
¾ pound of sugar
2 fifths dark rum
1 fifth brandy
6 ounces peach or apricot liqueur

Dissolve sugar in the water and lemon juice in a punch bowl. Pour in rum, brandy, and liqueur. Mix well. Add large block of ice, and allow to get good and cold. Stir thoroughly before serving.
Makes 50 four-ounce servings.

Eggnog

Beat yolks and whites of 8 eggs separately. Add ½ pound sugar to whites; beat until stiff. Combine beaten yolks and whites, and mix thoroughly. Add 3 ounces rum, and 1 fifth of whiskey or brandy. Beat mixture. Add 1 pint heavy cream, 1 quart milk. Mix. Chill well. Serve with a light sprinkling of nutmeg on top.
NOTE: if prepared eggnog is used, the proportions are: 2 parts mix to 1 part whiskey, rum, or brandy.
Makes 30 four-ounce servings.

Sangria Punch

1 bottle burgundy
2 large sliced lemons
2 sliced peaches
1 sliced orange
2 ounces Cointreau or Triple Sec
2 ounces brandy

Add sugar to taste, and club soda if desired.
Makes 6 servings.

Hot Buttered Rum

1 teaspoon sugar (white or brown)
1½ ounces rum
2 cloves
1 pat butter
Boiling water

Place sugar, rum, and cloves in a heavy mug or coffee cup. Fill with boiling water. Add butter and stir.

Plantation Punch

16 ounces orange juice
16 ounces lime juice
8 ounces pineapple juice
2½ cups grenadine
2 fifths Jamaica rum

Stir well, and pour into punch bowl with large piece of ice. Add slices of two oranges, maraschino cherries, quart of fresh cubed pineapple, or other available fruit.
Makes 40 four-ounce drinks.

Right: this guide will help you choose the wine that goes best with whatever food you're having.

A Guide to Food & Wine

Before dinner	enjoy a distinguished dry sherry, a cold sparkling white wine, or champagne.
With appetizers and soup	sip a chilled white wine.
With steaks, chops, roasts, and richer sauces	how about a dry, full-bodied red or rose wine.
With spaghetti or pasta	try a Chianti, Zinfandel, Grignolino, Burgundy, among many.
With chicken	some enjoy a red, others prefer a white wine. In either case, they should be dry: Claret, Burgundy, Graves, Riesling, Pinot Chardonnay, Italian Soave would all be delicious, among many others.
With roast beef	Burgundy is great; so is any other good, stout red wine.
With veal, pork, or ham	enjoy a dry, crisp white wine, a rose, or a dry, fruity red.
With fish, poultry, and shellfish dishes	go for a chilled dry, or semi-sweet white wine, or a rose.
With dessert, coffee, or after dining	choose a cream sherry, port, or sweet wine.

The Wedding:

The Bride (or her family) usually pays for:

- Invitations, announcements, and enclosure cards.
- Wedding dress, veil, accessories, and trousseau.
- Bouquets for maid of honor, bridesmaids, flower girl.
- Flowers for the church and reception.
- Engagement and wedding photographs.
- Rental fee (if any) for the church.
- Fees for the sexton, organist, and soloist.
- Rental of aisle carpet, marquee, or other equipment.
- Transportation of bridal party to church and reception.
- Reception, including food, beverages, music, decorations, and professional services (unless the groom's family offers to assume some of this cost).
- Groom's wedding ring (if it's a double-ring ceremony).
- Wedding gift for the groom.
- Gifts for bride's attendants.
- Lodging (if necessary) for out-of-town bridesmaids.
- Bride's personal stationery.

Either may or may not pay for:

- Bridesmaids' luncheon is usually given by the bride, but may be given by her attendants or relatives.
- Attendants' dresses are usually bought by each girl, but the bride may provide them if she wishes.

Who Pays for What?

It's well known that wedding expenses are heavier for the bride and her family than for the groom, but who is supposed to pay for what? This listing gives the traditional division of wedding costs.

The Groom (or his family) usually pays for:

- Bride's engagement and wedding rings.
- Marriage license.
- Clergyman's fee (can be from $10-$100; ask).
- Bride's flowers, including going-away corsage and bouquet (optional, see below).
- Boutonnières for the men of the wedding party.
- Corsages for mothers (see below).
- Gloves, ties, or ascots for men of the wedding party.
- Wedding gift for the bride.
- Complete wedding trip.
- Gifts for best man and ushers.
- Hotel accommodations (if any) for out-of-town ushers.

Either may or may not pay for:

- Bride's bouquet, traditionally a gift from the groom, may be purchased by bride's family as part of her outfit.
- Corsages for mothers and grandmothers are usually provided by the groom, but the bride may buy those for her own mother and grandmother.
- Bachelor dinner is given by groom in some areas, by his attendants and male friends in other localities.
- Rehearsal dinner is given by groom's family in many areas, but may be given by bride's family or friends.

Party Fun for Kids

When you plan a party for your children, keep their ages firmly in mind. One- and two-year-olds are altogether too young for a real party. Three-year-olds can enjoy one so long as it is kept simple and short. Four- and five-year-olds will appreciate organized games, such as musical chairs or pin-the-tail-on-the-donkey, a best-dressed contest, and some quiet activities for those who don't want to join in games. Competitive games, either

Left: paper plates and cups are convenient for any kind of party, but are practically essential for entertaining children. They cut the work for you, and make the children more relaxed about eating.

Below: little girls love a party for their dolls and stuffed animals, which should be seated at a table and served at the same time as their owners.

between teams or individuals, go over well at parties for seven- to 10-year-olds. They are ready, willing, and able to join in friendly competitions at these ages, and also have fun in the process.

☐ Line up paper bags with each guest's name on one at your young child's party. Favors, prizes, loose hair ribbons, and anything else that a child wants to save can be dropped into his or her bag as the party progresses. Then, each child will be able to carry away one tidy package—without forgetting something.

☐ A doll party is a favorite with small girls. Each guest brings her favorite doll as a guest, too. A small table is set for the dolls, complete with toy dishes and a few little cookies, so they can have refreshments when the girls do. Both the girls and the dolls also get favors.

☐ Collect all kinds of items from your

45

kitchen, living room, and garage, and spread them on the floor. One child, who is "it", must close his eyes, and while he does so, you remove one of the objects. See if he can guess which one you took.

☐ Little children become overexcited by too much organized play. To avoid this, have them arrive just when you are ready to serve the refreshments. Set the table with white paper mats on which you've drawn outlines of clowns, animals, or flowers. Place boxes of crayons at each place for favors, and let the children color the figures in while you are serving the food. It will keep them happily busy.

☐ Small children are sometimes frightened by being blindfolded. Allow them to cover their eyes with their hands instead.

☐ After a heavy snowfall is a good time for a children's party. Let the boys and girls make snowmen on the lawn to work off their excess energy, and then have them inside for refreshments. At each place setting, have a marshmallow snowman, made like this: make a paste of confectioner's sugar and a little milk, and use it to glue three marshmallows together, one on top of the other. Set these on a cooky base, and attach a cooky hat with a cherry on top. Add food coloring to the remaining paste, and paint a face on the snowman. Use wooden toothpicks for arms.

☐ For a delightful hot weather party, tell all the children to wear their bathing suits, turn on the sprinkler, and let the kids run through it. Serve sandwiches, lemonade, and ice cream cones on the lawn while they're drying off.

☐ A circus party is always fun for children. Decorate the table with balloons and animal crackers, and serve ice cream cones. Make clown hats with colored paper cones, or give the children instructions, and let them make the hats themselves.

☐ A balloon party: send invitations on inflated balloons with instructions painted on in nail polish. Deliver one to each guest at his home. At the party, have a balloon race in which contestants crawl along the floor pushing a balloon with their heads; a race in blowing up balloons; and a contest to see who can catch the most balloons when they are inflated with helium, tied with long strings, and allowed to float up to the ceiling.

☐ Older children like races of many kinds. Try filling two bags with the same articles of clothing in each. At a signal, two players race to be the first dressed. They must open their bag, put on all of the clothes inside, and close the bag.

☐ Six- to eight-year-old girls love to dress up in their mothers' old evening clothes. Let them get dressed up for a tea party, play some not-too-active games (so they won't trip on the long dresses), and do everything to make them feel grownup.

☐ Serve ice cream like this for a party change: put a paper cup or tin foil inside small new flower pots, and fill them with chocolate ice cream to simulate earth. Place a paper flower or a lollipop with paper leaves in the center of the ice cream.

☐ A gumdrop tree is a good centerpiece for a children's party. Take a bare branch that has a lot of twigs, and fasten it in a bowl with a lump of florist's clay. Attach gumdrops to the branches to look like flowers.

☐ A circus tent centerpiece can be made from a half circle of heavy paper about 22 inches in diameter. Roll and glue together to form a tent shape, leaving a little excess at the ends so that they can be folded back to make flaps. Place frosted animal crackers around the tent, holding them in place with toothpicks.

☐ To make a Jack Horner Pie for party favors, fill a large, shallow bowl with small wrapped gifts. Tie a ribbon to each one and lead it to a place setting. Cover the top of the bowl with foil or crepe paper, and place paper birds on top. After refreshments have been eaten, remove the cover, and let the children pull out their gifts by the ribbons.

☐ Decorate for an outdoor party by hanging balloons, party favors, lollipops, and paper flowers from a clothesline.

☐ Put the name of each guest on a paper cup with bright nail polish or paint. The cup can be a place card, and will also prevent mix-ups when refills are passed out.

Children's Etiquette

The best way to teach your child etiquette is to show him that you have consideration for others, and to encourage him to follow your example. You may think that good manners are too complicated and numerous to teach your child, but they are not. One set of manners is all you need—while your company manners may be slightly more formal than your everyday manners, the same rules still apply. Saying "please" and "thank you"; being prompt and neat; showing kindness and courtesy—these are the makings of good manners, and your child will acquire them simply by watching you. In the close confines of family living, manners are of the utmost importance. Each family member, no matter of what age, should learn to treat other members with respect and consideration. This way of getting along will then carry over to outside relationships.

☐ One of the essential points to get across in teaching your child manners is that courtesy is not extended only to those you like, and whom you want to like you. True good manners require courtesy to all: young and old, rich and poor, new acquaintances and old friends.

☐ A protest or criticism should be made quietly, courteously, and preferably in private. Your child should become aware as he matures that criticism should be given to improve a situation, not to give vent to temper or disappointment.

☐ Your son or daughter may sometimes use obscene language, even in public. You will do well not to overreact. The use of obscene language is often a child's way of testing you, of rebelling against your rules. If he fails to

Setting an example is the best way to teach etiquette to your children. If they see that you are courteous and considerate, they will follow suit.

get a rise out of you, he will amost always stop it.

☐ Give your child a small gift for the mother of his host or hostess when he is to be an overnight guest. If he is old enough, encourage him to select the gift himself, and to be thoughtful in making his selection. You might help with suggestions: packets of seed for a gardening enthusiast would be appreciated, for example, or a book of special interest. If your child visits the family often, he need not take a gift every time.

☐ "When in Rome, do as the Romans do" is the basic rule your child should learn before visiting other families. He should be prepared to follow the rules and customs of the family, even if they seem odd or unreasonable to him. If the family dog is meant to stay outdoors, he should not bring the pet into the living room. If the family gets up to have breakfast together, your child should get up and join the others. Explain that he can expect his house guests to follow your family rules, too, and this all may make a good deal more sense to him.

☐ Children should learn that proper introductions are an important way of making newcomers feel included. Set a good example by making friendly greetings a habit at home, and carefully introduce your children to strangers whenever there is occasion to. For practicing introductions, use the youngsters' stuffed animals and dolls, and keep things simple. The most an elementary school child needs to know is that men are introduced to women, and young people to older.

☐ Never spring the "social no" on your child. If he is allowed to eat chicken with his fingers at home, it is unfair to reprimand him for doing so when you are dining out. You must prepare him ahead of time, and explain why you are asking him to change his manners.

☐ Use a toy phone to practice telephone conversation with your child. Once he has learned to answer clearly and pleasantly, and not to leave a caller hanging, he can graduate to using the real thing.

☐ If your child should forget his manners in company, don't reprimand him in front of the guests. It will only frighten or embarrass him. Wait until you are alone; then explain what he should have done, and why.

☐ If your child has respect for family property, he will be more inclined to respect the property of others. He should become

Above: encourage your children to participate in games and sports more for the fun of it than for the idea of winning. Of course there is pleasure in winning, but it shouldn't be made all-important.

Left: to teach your child proper phone manners the easy way, practice on a toy telephone with her.

Right: if you consider your child old enough to sit at the table with the rest of the family, you should expect him to observe the same rules you do. This is the only way that dinner time will remain a family pleasure.

aware that his possessions are to be shared with his friends, and that he should take care of other's property, and return it promptly.

☐ Do not, through your own behavior, make your child feel that winning is all-important. The reason for participating in sports and games is enjoyment, and cut-throat competition is not fun. If your child wins, he is entitled to be pleased, but don't encourage him to give too much importance to winning. Instead, focus his attention on the pure enjoyment of the game.

☐ A child who is considered old enough to eat at the table should also be considered old enough to observe the rules that adults do.

Otherwise, you—and probably your child also—will only feel he is a problem at the table, rather than a welcome addition to the family. The basic rules are: no squirming or leaning on the table; eating silently and keeping his plate neat; and asking for dishes to be passed, rather than reaching across someone to get them.

☐ Your child should learn not to eat or drink in front of guests without offering them something too. This is one courtesy he will have an opportunity to use often, even if he is quite small.

☐ Elbows need not always be kept off the table—just when your child has a utensil in his hand. He should remember, however, that elbows should never go higher than the level of the table—even when cutting a tough piece of meat.

☐ You wouldn't grab your husband and pull him to the table if he wasn't ready when you called him for dinner, would you? Then don't do this with your children. They are entitled to advance notice before being asked to sit down for meals, as much as adults are. They also need a chance to wind down, and, when they get it, you may find them less inclined to sulk or squirm through dinner. By giving them a chance to prepare for dinner, you will also be encouraging them to put activities and possessions in some order before leaving them.

Making the Garden Grow

A pretty garden is something the whole family can enjoy, and gardening can also be a project for everyone to take part in. One of the easier things a young child can do is to help transplant flowers from pots to ground.

A hedge planted directly across the width of your garden, with an opening left in the center, will draw the eye through the first part of the grounds and into the second. This kind of landscaping will make grounds look larger.

Whether you're an avid gardener or a lazy one, a large-scale gardener or a window-box one, you're bound to find some helpful tips in the next pages. Here are suggestions not only about growing and caring for vegetables and flowers, but also about using them in unusual ways: vegetables as a border for a flower garden, for example, or trailing plants as a porch screen. There are also easy-to-do ideas on insect control, mulching, mowing and watering lawns, and rooting plant cuttings. Indoor plants, of course, come in for treatment, too—and you'll learn among other things how to keep your house plants happy while you're away on a longish trip; what causes leaves to yellow or blacken; and how to repot plants successfully.

☐ Carrots, leaf lettuce, parsley, beets, and radishes are vegetables that make pretty borders for flower gardens. With their delicate and feathery tops, carrots will make

50

your garden look like it is bordered with ferns.

☐ The new midget vegetables were created for gardeners short of space. They're as good—and sometimes better—than the standard size, they grow rapidly, and they can be crowded close together. Beets, cabbage, sweet corn, cucumbers, eggplant, lettuce, peas, peppers, pumpkin, squash, tomatoes, turnip, and watermelon are among those now available. You can even grow them in flower pots, if you like.

☐ Because potato plants bloom, they can make a pretty addition to your flower bed without seeming out of character.

☐ A vegetable garden is usually planted in one spot—but it doesn't have to be. Put tomatoes along a fence so they will climb rather than spread out along the ground, potatoes in a small strip along the drive, and peas in an unused corner of the yard. You may find you have more space than you imagined.

☐ Vegetables don't have to be grown in the ground. Fill old nail kegs, which you can probably get from your hardware dealer, or similar containers with soil, and plant your crop in them. The kegs can be used to line the driveway, or to separate a terrace from the rest of the yard.

☐ It may not seem likely, but six or seven tomato plants trained to grow up the sunny side of the garage will keep the average family well supplied with tomatoes all summer, and well into fall.

☐ The rule of thumb for the lazy gardener is to stick with plants that are easy to grow. Choose bibb lettuce and romaine over ice-

Above: roses must be properly pruned to keep them healthy and beautiful. The best time to do this is just after they bloom, although some pruning of dead stems may also be necessary in the spring.

berg lettuce. Broccoli will grow almost by itself, but cauliflower—which belongs to the same family—needs a great deal of care. Other easy growers are tomatoes, green peppers, squash, leaf lettuce, cucumbers, carrots, pumpkins, corn, peas, and snap beans. However, don't try to grow squash, pumpkin, or cucumber unless you have a large garden. Their spreading requires plenty of space.

☐ When you are short of both privacy and gardening space, try using plants as screens. For instance, you can shield a porch from clear view by hanging baskets of trailing ivy close together along the top.

☐ Use a waterproof cushion to sit and kneel on when gardening. An old pillow wrapped in plastic, an inflatable pillow, or a plastic coated car cushion are best.

☐ At the end of summer, mulch your row of carrots with hay, and you will be able to dig them throughout the winter, whenever you need some.

☐ Mulching is about the easiest way to cut down on weeds, but most mulches spoil the appearance of flower gardens. A dark mulch that is close to the color of the earth helps on appearance—coffee grounds and tea leaves with earth, rotted leaves, or wood ashes are a good mix.

☐ If the growing season is short in your area, don't set plants directly into window

Below: regular mowing of your lawn is important. If you let it get overgrown, and then hack it off, the lawn will be shocked and its growth retarded.

boxes. Leave them in their pots, and fill in the spaces between pots with peat moss or sphagnum. You will save soil as well as labor.

☐ Ladybugs eat 400 or more aphids in a week, so they can rid your garden of these pests virtually by themselves. Ladybugs usually arrive with the first warm weather, but they probably won't come into your garden if you have used chemical sprays in the past. However, you can purchase stock from a supplier. All you have to do is set the container of ladybugs down near the aphids, and dampen the surrounding soil.

☐ Praying mantises are another natural ally in keeping your garden insect free. They will

52

remain in your garden as long as there are enough insects to eat. Egg cases of praying mantises can be purchased between November and May. Tie the case to a tree, two-to-four feet above the ground. The eggs survive through the cold months, hatching out in June or July. Figure on five mantis egg cases for half an acre.

☐ One of the easiest ways to keep your garden free of insects is to plant insect repellent plants. Garlic and chives are the most popular, and they are easy to grow. Other plants good against insects are: nasturtiums (aphids), tansy (cutworms and cabbageworms), rue (all insects), and marigolds and asters (all insects to some degree). Rue is so repulsive to bugs that it will keep them off surrounding plants as well.

☐ Summer is the time to watch out for red spider mites. The leaves of a plant that is being attacked by this pest will look scratched and grayish, and may be covered with fine webs. Spider mites themselves are almost microscopic, but if you hold a piece of white paper under the plant and tap it, a few will probably fall onto the paper, and be spotted fairly easily.

☐ A spray of half a pound of laundry soap in two gallons of water will get rid of aphids, spider mites, red spiders, scale, and mealybugs. Wash the plants off after spraying. It may take several sprayings to eliminate the bugs entirely, but it's cheaper and safer than chemical sprays.

☐ New clay pots should be soaked in water overnight if you plan to put seedlings in them. Otherwise, the pots will draw off moisture from the soil.

☐ Plants that lean toward their source of light should be rotated a quarter turn each week. This will keep them from developing lopsidedly.

☐ The rocks you select for a rock garden should be of one kind and color to make the garden look unified and natural. In planning the garden, follow natural formations. Remember that light colored rocks tend to look artificial. Tilt rocks so water will flow down to plant roots.

☐ Since perennials last for years, they will be one of the foundations of your garden. Starting perennials from seed is cheaper than buying small plants, but much more difficult.

☐ Choosing a good site is one way of keeping garden work to a minimum. Avoid low areas where the soil will remain soggy after the rains, and areas that do not receive at least six hours of direct sun a day. Try not to plant on subsoil fill, or near big trees or shrubs, which will usually take moisture and nutrients the garden plants need.

☐ When planting in shady spots, allow more space between plants, as in nature. Besides looking more natural, well spaced plants

Water hanging plants more often than potted ones, because they dry out faster. Be sure to put them in easy-to-reach spots, and attach them firmly.

can make better use of side and reflected light than crowded ones. They will also be able to spread their foliage to get the greatest amount of light from above.

☐ There are no hard and fast rules about when to water your lawn. As a guide, however, and in the absence of rainfall, lawns in sandy, fast draining soils should be watered about every three days, and those in heavier, clay-type soils every four or five days.

☐ There are often hot spots in lawns, usually next to walks, curbs, or driveways. These spots may lose color sooner than other areas, and thus warn you that the entire lawn needs watering.

☐ You should mow your lawn at least once a week, preferably when the grass is dry. Mowing every four or five days in growing season is advisable, so that you do not cut off too much of the plants in one mowing. If you should go away on vacation, or fall behind your mowing schedule for some other reason, the grass may grow quite tall. In such cases, raise the cutting height of your mower to avoid taking too big a bite out of the grass.

☐ During the winter months, avoid walking over grass that has become frosted, or you will crush the frozen cells of the grass blades, and black footprints will result. These disappear only very slowly.

☐ The easy way to destroy grass growing in sidewalk cracks: pour a little gasoline over it.

☐ While you are waiting for cuttings from your favorite plants to root, keep them in a decorative arrangement by using the foam block most florists use. This foam not only can hold the cuttings, but can also be shaped into a design. When the cuttings have put out roots, the foam can be crumbled, leaving the new roots intact and undamaged. Foam block can be purchased at florists and variety stores in different sizes and colors.

☐ Plant cuttings of your favorite plants in a paper cup. When the cutting is ready to be transplanted, simply tear away the cup. You can then transplant without disturbing the new roots.

☐ When you are going to be away from

Potted plants will thrive better if the water you use on them has been allowed to stand for about a day. This is because chlorine is not good for house plants, and letting tap water stand reduces the chlorine content of it.

Right: if you find that it's hard to clean your hands after you've been working in the soil, rub them with slightly moistened soap before starting a gardening session.

home for six weeks or so, you can keep plants watered by this method: water and drain as usual, and then stick three stakes slightly taller than the plant into the soil, spacing them evenly around the pot. Slant the tops outward. Put a plastic bag over the plant, making sure the stakes keep the plastic from touching the leaves. Draw the bag around the bottom of the pot, and fasten with a rubber band to make the seal airtight. Place the plants in direct light. When you return, open your mini-greenhouse for just a couple of hours the first day, a few more the second, and so on, until your plant has readjusted to the normal environment of the house. You can usually remove the bag for good on the fourth day.

☐ You can have flowering plants in your home even without direct sun. Spathiphyllum (spathe flower) has fragrant white flowers, blooms easily, and doesn't require direct sunlight.

☐ A good way to make sure that house

plants have a humid environment is to place the pots in a plastic or metal tray filled with pebbles and water. In this way they receive the humidity of evaporating water without getting excess water through the hole in the bottom of the pot. Buy trays that fit shelves or window sills, and that are $1\frac{1}{2}$ to two inches deep. Trays may also be placed on top of radiators, if insulating material is placed between the tray and the radiator.

☐ Rub the leaves of your house plants with a little mineral oil to give them a nice gloss.

☐ It is best to water house plants in the morning. Lingering moisture and cooler temperatures at night make the plant prone to fungus disease.

☐ Plants kept in bathrooms should be fungus and mildew resistant. Try grape ivy, Boston fern, bromeliads, and English ivy. They are all strong, and able to grow in a humid atmosphere with minimum light.

☐ One of the mistakes made most often in repotting house plants is to use too large a pot. Plants do better if the roots are somewhat constricted, so, under ordinary circumstances, it is best to use pots only one size larger than the previous one for transplanting.

☐ If you find the leaves of your house plants yellowing, you are probably overwatering them. Overwatering robs soil of its nutrients, so you should repot a plant that was watered too much.

☐ Whitish or yellow-brown spots on leaves usually mean the plant is receiving too much sun.

☐ Exposure to extremes of temperature will cause the leaves of house plants to blacken. Too little fertilizer or light are other possible causes.

☐ Plants that grow spindly are usually not getting enough light. Move your plant to a sunnier location, and it should develop a full, bushy shape.

☐ If your home is too drafty, dry, or dark for house plants, don't give up all thought of having some indoor greenery. Put your plants in bottles. Clear or lightly tinted bottles trap moisture, and create the humid, draft-free environment that plants like. A gallon bottle garden requires only a tablespoon of water every three or four months, which means you needn't worry if you go away and there's no one to water plants for you.

☐ Bottle gardens must be clean, or they will develop growths of fungus inside. Use sterilized packaged soil when starting one, and rinse out the bottle with very hot water and a strong household disinfectant. Another precaution is to spray the leaves of the plants with rubbing alcohol.

☐ To construct a floor garden, arrange a large tray, or several small trays of varying sizes, on the floor. Fill the trays with potted plants. Smaller plants should be toward the front of the display, so they will hide the pots of taller plants behind them. A pool can be made simply by partitioning off one part of the big tray, or using one small tray.

General Tips, Hints, and Shortcuts

Here is a handy grab-bag of miscellaneous tips and hints with a little bit about a lot of things, from bargain hunting to making a move, from burglar-proofing your home to heating and cooling it more economically. Just dip in and pull out a surprising suggestion for a furniture polish substitute, an easy way to repair cigarette burns in carpets, a happy answer to the problem of tight toes in shoes, or an ingenious method of wrapping gifts safely for mailing. These are pages you might browse through just for the fun of it, or, on the other hand, refer to for something specific. In any case, you will find helpful, simple, and practical ideas you can put to use.

☐ Watch for sales held by regional post offices and police departments. The Post Office auctions off damaged items on which it has paid insurance claims, and the police offer nonreturnable stolen goods. Who knows what treasure you may find? Post Office auctions are held twice a year, and police sales about once a year.

☐ Turn off lights even when you are leaving the room for only a short time. Many people think that turning lights on and off frequently uses a lot of electricity. This is not true. It costs virtually nothing to switch lights on and off.

☐ To save on your electric bill, use florescent lighting where you can. Florescent bulbs last longer, and use less power.

☐ Leaky faucets, especially hot water ones, are expensive. The Office of Consumer Affairs says that just a drop per second adds up to 700 gallons a year. Repair those leaks.

☐ Although they are not cheap to install, storm windows and doors save so much on heating bills that they usually pay for themselves in six or seven years. Most homes lose more than 25 per cent of their heat through the windows, and storm windows can cut this figure in half.

☐ Heating, cooling, and hot water account for at least 50 per cent of your utility bill, so any economizing on these can cut your bill significantly. A few easy ways to save are: don't run your dishwasher, washing machine, or dryer with less than a full load; don't let the hot water run steadily while you do the dishes; keep room temperature slightly below 70 degrees for the greatest economy, and turn down the thermostat at night.

☐ If you have many books to move, you will save money by mailing them at the special fourth class book rate, rather than having the mover transport them.

☐ Among the most irksome noises in your home are those made by electric blenders and mixers. To muffle them, place such appliances on rubber sink mats.

☐ When your washing machine or dishwasher overflows, sprinkle salt over the suds. They will disappear immediately.

☐ Blockage of water pipes is often due to lint from your washing machine. To keep pipes practically lint-free, slip an old nylon stocking over the drain hose, letting the foot hang free, and anchor the leg with a tight rubber band at the end of the hose. The stocking will trap lint that otherwise would flow down the drain with the rinse water, thus preventing blockage.

☐ Toes of shoes that are too tight can be stretched by stuffing them with wet newspaper. Crumple newspaper into balls, wet it, and stuff the toes of the shoes very tightly. Let the stuffing stay in the shoes at least a few

56

Left: make big savings on your gas bill by steering clear of higher priced name brands. Most gas is of the same quality, so simply buy the cheapest.

Below: the stalls of the Lower East Side of New York offer many a bargain to the smart shopper. Look around your own hometown for bargain areas.

Left: the best way to keep leaves out of your gutters is to cover them with plastic wire screening. It's inexpensive and durable. Don't use metal screening; it will rust.

Right: yard goods, like manufactured products, must have care labels to tell you how to get the most wear out of them by proper care. Ask for care labels when you buy fabric for home sewing, and sew them firmly into the clothes you have made.

days—or, better still, a week if possible.
☐ The best time to buy a new pair of shoes is when you are tired, and have been on your feet for some time. Your feet will be more sensitive at this time, and perhaps even swollen. Therefore, if a pair of shoes feels comfortable when your feet are tired, chances are they will feel good under most other circumstances, too.
☐ If you wash windows in freezing weather, use two tablespoons of glycerine or alcohol in the wash and rinse waters. This helps to keep the glass from steaming up.
☐ Use a windshield wiper to dry windows after they are clean. Hold the wiper flat against the glass, and pull down in a straight line. Dry the wiper after each stroke.
☐ Don't wash windows when the sun shines directly on them. The glass will dry too quickly.
☐ Empty your vacuum cleaner bag into a *wet* paper bag, and there will be a lot less dust flying around.
☐ Before vacuuming, put three or four cloves into a fresh vacuum cleaner bag. A clean, spicy scent will be left wherever you vacuum. It's more pleasant and cheaper than air fresheners you buy in spray cans.
☐ Make the packages you mail secure and tight by tying them with wet string. Wet string will shrink as it dries, and hold the package more tightly.
☐ To insure against breakage when packing gifts to be mailed, choose an outer box at least two inches larger on all sides than the gift you plan to enclose. Fill the space around the gift with popcorn on all sides; the popcorn will absorb shocks and jolts.
☐ Make a wooden rack to keep your stemware tidy. Cut dowels of $\frac{1}{2}$ inch diameter into pieces $3\frac{1}{2}$ inches long. Glue them to a strip of wood, spacing them to fit the glass stems exactly. Paint the rack a bright color, or leave it in natural wood. It doesn't take much space, but is very handy.
☐ If your candles are slightly too big for your candlesticks, heat the bottom end of the candle over a flame, or dip it in hot water for a few seconds, and fit it in the holder while the wax is still warm. For the opposite problem of a candlestick hole that is too large, use florist's clay around the candle to hold it in.
☐ If odors linger inside plastic containers,

wash them in hot sudsy water, rinse, dry, and put a piece of crumpled newspaper inside. Seal and leave overnight. The ink and porous paper absorbs the odor. Just remember not to use magazines or color sections, which are not absorbent.

☐ To clean a narrow necked bottle or vase, break up some egg shell. Push it into the bottle, add water, shake, and rinse. The shells will dislodge the grime in the neck.

☐ To clean copper pots, make a paste of salt and vinegar. Rub on with a sponge or dishcloth, and rinse.

☐ Upholstery fabrics with thick threads running one way and thin threads the other, are almost always a bad buy. Fabrics woven in this manner tend to develop slits in them because the thin threads wear through before the thick ones.

☐ Cigarette burns in carpets can be repaired. With a razor blade, slice off a few tufts from a part of the carpet under the sofa, or in some other unobtrusive place. Rub a little Elmer's Glue into the burnt spot, and sprinkle the tufts over it. Press down with your fingers.

☐ If you run out of furniture polish and are in need of a quick replacement, a bit of mayonnaise rubbed on with a soft cloth will do the trick.

☐ When you finish defrosting the freezer, cover the bottom of it with a sheet of plastic wrap. When it is time to defrost again, simply pick up the plastic, and the frost will come up with it.

☐ Ice cube trays should not be washed in hot water or strong detergent. Both of these will remove the nonstick finish of the tray.

☐ If you don't have enough room to store place mats in your kitchen cabinets, clip them onto a clipboard. They can then be hung on the inside of a cabinet, or, to brighten your kitchen, on the wall.

☐ When your cedar chest loses its scent, sand the inside lightly, and it will smell like new again.

☐ Clippings may be ironed instead of pasted into your scrapbook. Simply cut a piece from a plastic cleaner's bag, and trim it to the same size as the clipping. Put the plastic between the page and the clipping, and run over it with a heated iron. The iron should be hot enough to melt the plastic, but not hot enough to scorch the paper.

59

☐ Next time you have the windshield wipers on your car changed, save one of the old ones. It will be useful for wiping away fog on the *inside* of the windshield.

☐ To start a new ball of yarn in the middle of a row of knitting, unravel about an inch of yarn both at the end of the old ball and at the start of the new one, moisten them, and roll them together between the palms of your hand. This way the ends are firmly joined without an unsightly knot.

☐ Mending a knitted garment will be easier if you place the torn part over the bristles of a hairbrush. In this way, the material will not slip or stretch as you work on it.

☐ To keep buttons with metal shanks from falling off coats, sew them on with dental floss instead of thread. It's much stronger.

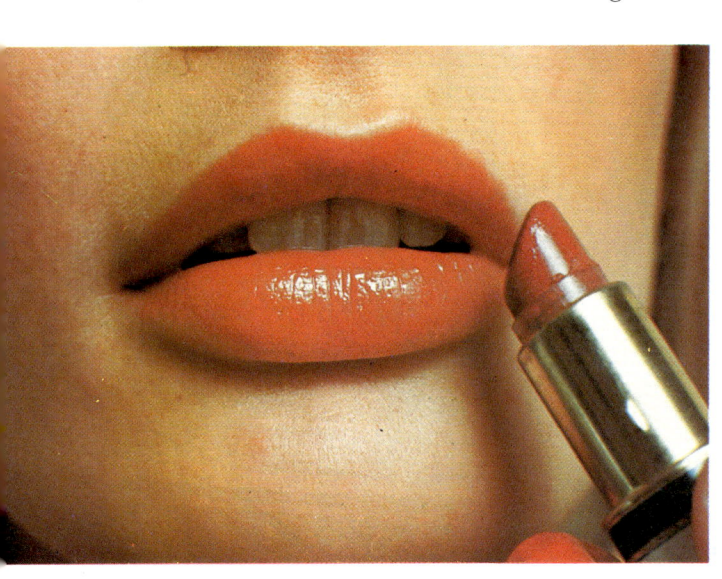

☐ Place a short strip of masking tape next to your sewing machine, sticky side up. It is useful for holding bits of threads you clip off. When you have finished sewing, simply throw out the tape. A magnet is good for picking up stray pins.

☐ Place one end of your ironing board over the bed when you iron anything of long length. The end of the long dress or curtains will then end up on the bed, not on the floor.

☐ Place a rubber mat in front of your fuse box to lessen the chance of getting a shock, especially if it's in the cellar with unfinished floors. Concrete floors tend to become damp, which is dangerous when dealing with electricity.

☐ The head restraints attached to the top of car seats are safety devices, but all too often they are not properly adjusted. The top of the cushion should never be lower than the tops of the passenger's or driver's ears, and no more than one to six inches behind the head.

☐ Bee and wasp nests should be destroyed at night, not during the day. This is because lower temperatures make the insects less active. If you must use a flashlight, do not point it directly at the nest, or it will attract the insects.

☐ The "back to nature" trend in cosmetics is confusing some consumers. Unscented

Left: even cosmetics that are labeled "hypoallergenic" may still contain some allergens, of which about 60 could be present. Check the label carefully to find out if any chemicals that irritate you are present in the product.

Right: the correct shoe fitting for children is vitally important to their general well-being. Try to buy shoes for your child in a store known for fitting consultation.

products are not necessarily hypoallergenic, (less likely to cause allergic reactions) and even those that are may still contain some allergens. There are approximately 60 allergens that could be present in your beauty products, and how many of them must be eliminated to warrant the name "hypoallergenic" is not definite. There are no government regulations fixing standards in this area, so you should check the label on all cosmetics you buy to determine whether any chemicals irritating to you are present.

☐ One of the best ways to discourage burglars—even if they have already broken into your home—is to mark all of your valuables with your driver's license, Social Security, or phone number, or your name. Operation Identification, a nationwide program supported by many local civic groups and police departments, recommends that you register these numbered items with police. The best way to mark items is to use an electric engraving pen, which hobby shops sell for as little as $7.50, and which come with a decal for your window or door that reads: "All items of value on these premises are marked for ready identification by law enforcement agencies." These decals have proven to be an effective deterrent to burglars. If there is no Operation Identification office in your area, follow the recommendations of the National Association of Insurance Agents.

☐ The U.S. Food and Drug Administration advises that you buy a baby crib with slats no more than $2\frac{3}{8}$ inches apart. A baby's body can slip through slats spaced wider than this, and lead to injury or strangulation. Also be sure your crib mattress is large enough to fit the crib frame. Otherwise, the child could suffocate by slipping into the space between the mattress and the side of the crib.

☐ A survey of pediatricians indicates that special shoes for babies are a waste of money, and of no value in aiding the normal growth of an infant's foot. Well-fitted sneakers are just as acceptable for the baby with no foot problems as high-top leather shoes, which may cost from $10 to $15. For further information, send for a handbook put out by the American Medical Association. It will answer many of your questions concerning child care.

☐ Toddlers' shoelaces seem to come untied a hundred times a day. Besides the inconvenience, trailing shoelaces can result in a bad fall. To keep laces tied, purchase a small spring binder clip at a stationery store, and clip it over the knot of each lace. It keeps the knot from coming undone, and most toddlers are not strong enough to unclamp it.

☐ Talcum powder, although certainly less dangerous than many substances found in the average kitchen or bathroom, should be kept out of reach of toddlers. Inhaling quantities of spilled talcum powder has caused the deaths of a number of one- and two-year-olds by suffocation.

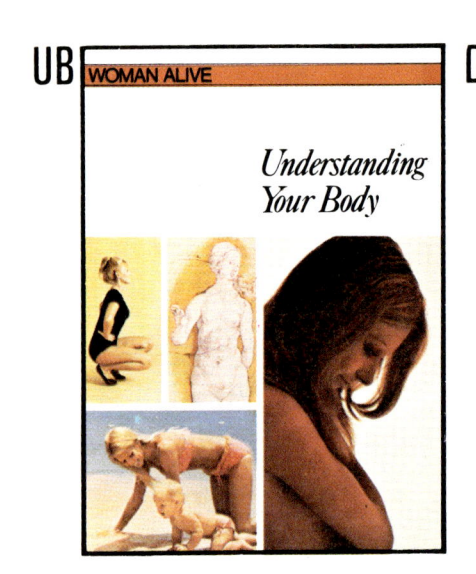

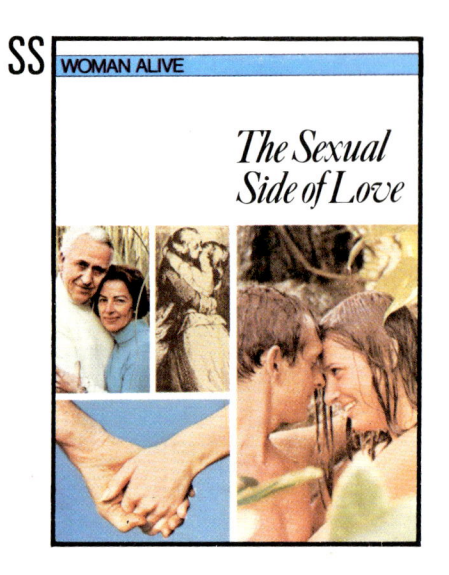

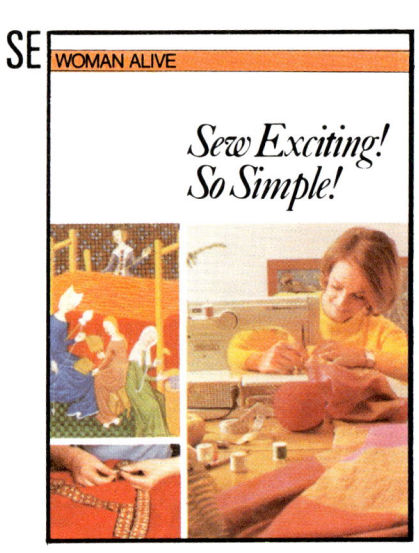

UB WOMAN ALIVE *Understanding Your Body*	**DL** WOMAN ALIVE *Discover a Lovelier You*	**SS** WOMAN ALIVE *The Sexual Side of Love*
GF WOMAN ALIVE *Guarding Your Family's Health*	**SE** WOMAN ALIVE *Sew Exciting! So Simple!*	**HD** WOMAN ALIVE *How to Decorate Without Going Broke*
FL WOMAN ALIVE *Food for Life, Love, and Looks*	**PY** WOMAN ALIVE *A Paycheck of Your Own*	**TW** WOMAN ALIVE *Talking with Your Child*

The letter code shown on these two pages will help you use this index to all 18 books of Woman Alive. When you see one of these codes in front of a page reference, it tells you which book to look in for that particular page. The letter code is conveniently repeated throughout the index.

Index

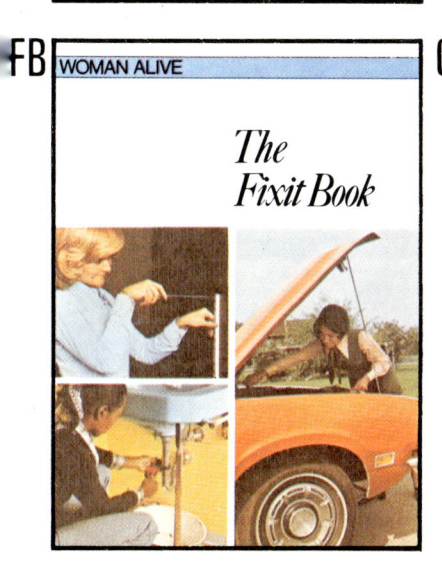

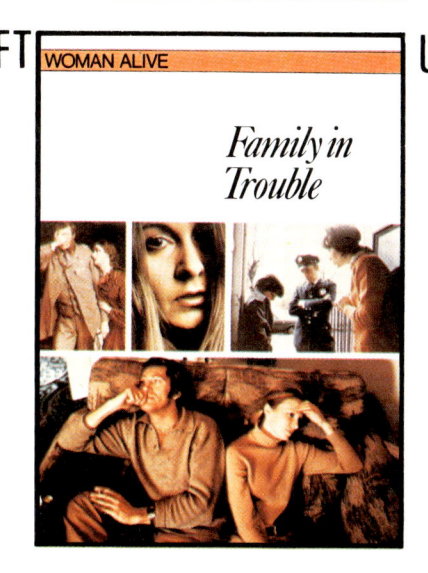

WM — What Makes Men Tick

CF — Crafts for Fun and Profit

YM — Your Money's Worth

FB — The Fixit Book

OY — On Your Own

KS — Key to Self-Understanding

GF — Guide to Travel and Recreation

FT — Family in Trouble

UT — Useful Tips, Hints, and Shortcuts & INDEX

Abdomen

Achievement

Abdomen, exercises for, **DL** 102-103
Abortion, advice and information, **FT** 135;
Clergy Consultation Service on, **FT** 57;
Emotional aftermath, **FT** 60, **SS** 101; in birth control, **SS** 100; in the teenager, **FT** 57; law on, **FT** 135
Abrasive mitts, **DL** 76
ABS, **UT** 21
Academic pressure, on the teenager, **TW** 117
Accessories, fashion, **DL** 126;
in home decorating, **HD** 87
Accident, automobile, first aid in, **GF** 143; in the home, **GF** 88
Accommodation, vacation, **GT** 30, 51
Accomplishments, in personal inventory, **PY** 52
Accosting of the single woman, **OY** 143
Accountancy, for women, **PY** 132
Accounting Careers Council, **PY** 132
Acetate, **HD** 139
Achievement, age for, **GF** 78

Acne

Acne, **DL** 34 ; **FL** 121 ; **GF** 44 ; dermabrasion for, **DL** 139
Acoustical tiles, **HD** 136
Acrylic, **HD** 140 ; sheet plastic, **UT** 21
Activities, extra-occupational, in avoidance of stress, **GF** 70
Adaptability of woman, **KS** 22
AdapTable, **HD** 104
Adhesive-backed hangers, **FB** 38
Adhesives, what sticks what, **UT** 20 (table)
Adirondack Mountain Club, **GT** 76
Adjustable crescent wrench, **FB** 26, 27
Adolescence. *See also* Teenage(rs) calorie requirements, **FL** 22, 23 ; love in, **WM** 92, masturbation in, **TW** 139 ; problems of, **FT** 10-11 ; **GF** 41 ; sexual awareness in, **WM** 51 ; social pressure in, **FT** 76, stress in, **FT** 112 ; unsocial behavior, **FT** 43
Adoption of child, by parent's remarriage partner, **OY** 123 ; effect on natural mother, **FT** 59 ; procedure, **FT** 136
Adoption Resource Exchange of North America (ARENA), **FT** 137
Adrenalin, **UB** 38, 40
Adultery, benefit of, to some marriages, **SS** 56, 81 ; effect on the marriage partner, **SS** 55
Adulthood, criterion of, **TW** 123 (table)
Advanced schedule flights, **GT** 91
Adventure Trip Guide, **GT** 77
Adventure, need for, in teenage, **FT** 48 ; vacations, **GT** 60
Adversity, precursor to happiness, **KS** 125
Advertising, career prospects for women, **PY** 138 ; for marketing of crafts, **CF** 139, 140 ; ideal woman of, **KS** 106 ; pressures of, **KS** 113
Aerobics, **DL** 104
Aerosol foam, contraceptive, **SS** 97
AFDC (Aid to Families with Dependent Children), **OY** 136
Affirmative action programs, **PY** 90, 91
Age, best for facelift, **DL** 136 ; in exercise program, **UB** 100 ; of achievement, **GF** 78
Agencies, child care, **PY** 114 ; counseling, **FT** 24 ; **PY** 54 ; employment, commercial, **PY** 65
Agency, employment, state, **PY** 66 ; employment, temporary, **PY** 34
Aggression in the young child, role of play in management of, **TW** 63 ; role of, in relief of tension, **UB** 56
Aging process, **GF** 79 ; **UB** 136 ; and sexual appetite, **SS** 118, 120 ; reasons for, **UB** 136 ; sex differences, **UB** 137
Aid to Families with Dependent Children (AFDC), **OY** 136
Air conditioners, buying of, **YM** 70 ; home, **FB** 140
Air fares, long-distance, **GT** 91
Air freshening, by vacuum cleaner, **UT** 58
Air ticket, loss of, procedure, **GT** 141
Air travel, baby needs, **GT** 139 ; for the pregnant woman, **GT** 133
Al-Anon Family Groups, **FT** 92
Alateen groups, **FT** 92
Alcohol and the Adolescent, **FT** 132
Alcohol, calorie values, **GF** 64-65 ; effects, **FT** 87 (table) ; **UB** 88 ; effect on complexion, **DL** 32 ; excess, effect of, **TW** 143 ; **UB** 10 ; excess, in adolescence, **GF** 52 ; in reducing, **GF** 60 ; stain, removal, **UT** 22 ; synergism with barbiturates, **UB** 92
Alcoholic, definition, **FT** 86
Alcoholics Anonymous, **FT** 88
Alcoholism, age factor, **FT** 82 ; as an illness, **FT** 85 ; causes, **FT** 86 ; cure of, family's supporting role, **FT** 92 ; companies' rehabilitation of employees, **FT** 86 ; differentiation from heavy drinking, **FT** 86 ; gauge of, **UB** 86 ; helping agencies, **FT** 132 ; in teenagers, **FT** 131 ; in women, **UB** 87, 90 ; incidence, **UB** 90 ; signs of, **FT** 84, 88 ; stages in decline and recovery, **FT** 90-91 ; statistics **FT** 81 ; through the ages, **FT** 12-13
Alexander Graham Bell Association for the Deaf, **FT** 140
Alimony, **OY** 134
Allergens, in cosmetics, **UT** 61
Alteration of pets, **UT** 10
Aluminum windows,

Aluminum windows

65

Ambition

maintenance, **FB** 95
Ambition, effect on man's home life, **WM** 64; male attribute, **WM** 63; of parent for teenager, **TW** 116; of wife for husband, **WM** 141
American Academy of Matrimonial Lawyers, **FT** 137
American Antique Association, **GT** 30
American Association of Advertising Agencies, **PY** 138
American Association of Junior Colleges, **PY** 130
American Association of Marriage and Family Counselors, **FT** 137; **PY** 131
American Association of Mental Health Counselors, **PY** 132
American Board of Plastic Surgery, **DL** 131
American Camping Association, **OY** 69; **PY** 122
American Cancer Society, **GF** 78
American Crafts Council, **GT** 29
American Dental Hygienists Association, **PY** 136
American Dietetic Association, **PY** 136
American Forestry Association camping club, **GT** 46, 77
American Heart Association, **GF** 78
American Home Economics Association, **PY** 136
American Institute of Architects, **PY** 137
American Institute of Planners, **PY** 138
American Kitefliers Association, **GT** 126
American Marketing Association, **PY** 133
American Medical Association, **DL** 131; **PY** 134
American Newspaper Publishers Association, **PY** 141
American Occupational Therapy Association, **PY** 135
American Physical Therapy Association, **PY** 136
American School Counselor Association, **PY** 132
American Society of Clinical Pathologists, **PY** 135
American Society of Landscape Architects, **PY** 137
American Society of Travel Agents, **GT** 92; **PY** 139
American Speech and Hearing Association, **FT** 140; **PY** 135
American Translators Association, **PY** 142
American Youth Hostels Inc., **GT** 77
Amino acids, in cosmetics, **FL** 126
Amish people, **GF** 11
Amphetamine abuse, **FT** 70, 73 (table); **UB** 91
Amulets, Egyptian, **UB** 12
Amusement of the sick child, **GF** 112 (table), 116
ANA-NLN Committee on Nursing Careers, **PY** 134
Anatomy, ancient, **UB** 6, 7; modern aids to learning, **UB** 7
Anchors, expansion-type, **FB** 38
Anger, brain-body relationship, **UB** 41; how to work off, **UB** 56
Anidex, **HD** 139
Animals, dreams of, **UB** 132; farms, **GT** 114
Ankles, exercises for, **DL** 114-115
Anorexia nervosa, **FL** 137
Antabuse, **FT** 84
Antibodies, **UB** 63
Antioxidants, in foods, **FL** 41
Antiperspirants, **DL** 76, **UB** 125
Antique finishing, **HD** 63
Antique Hunters' vacations, **GT** 30
Antiseptics, **GF** 131
Anti-tetanus injection, **GF** 131
Ants, control of, **FB** 135
Anxiety in, **KS** 140; **TW** 130. *See also* Stress
Apartments, **OY** 142; **YM** 88. *See also* Condominium living
Aperitif buffet, **UT** 29
Appalachian Mountain Club, **GT** 77
Appalachian trail, **GT** 110
Appestat, **DL** 84; **UB** 75
Appetite, coaxing, of the sick child, **FL** 131; lack of, due to anorexia nervosa, **FL** 137; poor, eating pattern for, **FL** 94; suppressants, **DL** 83; **FL** 138
Apples, health-giving properties, **UB** 15
Appliances, home, checking before repair, **FB** 72; buying of, **YM** 64, 71-73; plug, **FB** 63
Application letter for job, **PY** 66-69
Applique, definition, **SE** 136
Apron, barbecue, **SE** 101
Archeological digs, **GT** 86
Architecture, training in, **PY** 137
Arms, batwing, cosmetic surgery for, **DL** 143; exercises for, **DL** 96-97

Art of loving

Art of loving, **SS** 126

Arthritis Foundation

Arthritis Foundation, **GF** 78
Arts-and-Crafts vacations, **GT** 29, 80
Ascorbic acid, food additive, **FL** 41
Asphalt tiling, **HD** 47
Aspirin, hazards of, **UB** 84
Association for Voluntary Sterilization, **SS** 100
Association of American Publishers Inc., **PY** 142
Atheroma, **FL** 100, 102
Atherosclerosis, **FL** 100, 102
At-home work for the single woman, **OY** 54
Atlanta-Montreal vacation trip, **GT** 28
Attached salary, **OY** 136
Attic, periodic inspection, **FB** 133
Auction sale, **YM** 60-61
Auger, closet, **FB** 57; hand, **FB** 28
Austrian shades, **HD** 53
Authority of parent, teenager's challenge of, **TW** 100
Authorization for medical treatment, **GF** 143
Auto Tape Tour, **GT** 30
Automobiles, accident, first aid in, **GF** 143; breakdown, by the single woman, **OY** 143; buying of, **YM** 70, 74; buying abroad and shipping home, **GT** 132; bargaining, **YM** 78; trade-in traps, **YM** 76; checking for vacation, **GT** 32-33; depreciation of, **YM** 70; diagnostic clinic, **YM** 75; family, use of by teenagers, **TW** 107; insurance. *See* Insurance, auto; maintenance, **FB** 119, 123; on vacation, **GT** 24; over the years, **FB** 12-13; ownership, economics of, **YM** 70; rise in, **YM** 74 (graph); yearly cost of, **YM** 74 (chart); recreational vehicle, **GT** 38; rental in Europe, **GT** 141; repairs, excessive charges, **YM** 142; secondhand, checking before buying, **YM** 74, 76-77; law on, **YM** 75; systems, **FB** 124, 125; theft and burglary, **GT** 35; travel, recommended daily maximum mileage, **GT** 27
Automobile Association of America, **GT** 27, 32
Autonomic nervous system, **UB** 40
Awl, hand, **FB** 35

Ax

Ax, scout, **FB** 93

Code Key		
CF:	Crafts for Fun and Profit	
DL:	Discover a Lovelier You	
FB:	The Fixit Book	
FL:	Food for Life, Love, and Looks	
FT:	Family in Trouble	
GF:	Guarding Your Family's Health	
GT:	Guide to Travel and Recreation	
HD:	How to Decorate Without Going Broke	
KS:	Key to Self-Understanding	
OY:	On Your Own	
PY:	A Paycheck of Your Own	
SE:	Sew Exciting! So Simple!	
SS:	The Sexual Side of Love	
TW:	Talking With Your Child	
UB:	Understanding Your Body	
UT:	Useful Tips, Hints, and Shortcuts	
WM:	What Makes Men Tick	
YM:	Your Money's Worth	

Baby

Ballpoint inkstain

Baby(ies), accident in the home **GF** 90 ; christening gown, **SE** 61 ; coat, **SE** 65 ; communication of love to, **TW** 26 development patterns, **TW** 36-37 ; differing characters, **TW** 30 ; dress, **SE** 69 ; first words, **TW** 33 ; layette, **SE** 61-69 ; new arrival, effect on young school child, **TW** 72 ; new, explanation to the older child, **TW** 132 ; nightgown, **SE** 69
Baby-sitter, child's getting used to, **TW** 131

Bachelorhood, drawbacks of, **WM** 106
Backpacking, **GT** 109
Backstitch, definition, **SE** 136
Bag, shoulder-, macrame, **CF** 115
Bait-and-switch selling, **YM** 142
Bakeries, "day-old" shops, **UT** 7
Balance, in room arrangement, **HD** 71
Ballcock repairs, **FB** 53
Balloon(s), in mobile-making, **CF** 122-124 ; party, **UT** 46
Ballpoint inkstain, removal, **UT** 23

Bank(s)

Bank(s) **YM** 10-11 ; as insurance agents, **YM** 113 ; by-mail, **YM** 23 ; charges, **YM** 21 ; checking accounts, **YM** 21 ; choice of, **YM** 22 ; commercial, advantages, **YM** 25 ; credentials, **YM**, 24 ; credit cards, **YM** 52
Barbecue apron, **SE** 101
"Barbie" dolls, clothes for, **SE** 125
Barbiturate(s), abuse, **FT** 71, 72 (table) ; **UB** 91 ; synergism with alcohol, **UB** 92 ; variety of color and shape, **UB** 88-89
Bargain calendar, **YM** 80-81
Bargaining on vacation, **GT** 131
Basement, inspection, **FB** 133 ; windows, dressing, **HD** 55
Baste, definition, **SE** 136 ; machine, **SE** 138
Bath, beauty, **DL** 73 ; essence, **DL** 75 ; robe, doll's, **SE** 130
Bathing, **UB** 14, 124
Bathroom, decoration, **HD** 133 ; floor coverings, **HD** 40 ; lighting, **HD** 82
Batik work, **CF** 74-79
Battered child, the, **FT** 141
Battery, dead, of car, **FB** 120
Bay windows, dressing, **HD** 53
Beach charges in Europe **GT** 132
Beach tote, **SE** 33
Bead necklaces, **CF** 27-35 ; marketing of, **CF** 138 ; materials, **CF** 27 ; stringing, 28-29
Beads, polystyrene, for cushion chair, **SE** 113
Beauty, changing concepts, **FL** 115 ; foods for, **DL** 90 ; ingredients for, **DL** 24 ; of fitness, **FL** 115 ; **UB** 94 ; woman's search for, **DL** 16
Beds, bunk, **HD** 22, 114 ; camping, **GT** 40 ; choice of, **HD** 59 ; convertible, **HD** 60 ; dog, **UT** 12 ; four-poster, in small room, **HD** 131
Bed rest, for sick children, **GF** 111
Bedbugs, control of, **FB** 135
Bedroom fireplaces treatment, **HD** 133 ; floor coverings, **HD** 39 ; furniture arrangement, **HD** 71 ; lighting, **HD** 82
Bedspread of fake fur, **SE** 77
Bed-wetting, in the school starter, **TW** 64
Bee nest, destruction, **UT** 60
Beef, cooking economics, **YM** 28 ; cuts of, and cooking methods, **YM** 31 ; shopping for, **YM** 27
Beer for hair care, **DL** 58 ; in cooking, **UT** 9
Beeswax candles, **CF** 54, 55
Beetle, carpet, control of, **FB** 135
Behavior, awkward, in the young child, **TW** 46 ; of children under stress, **FT** 110 ; problems of the teenager, **FT** 45 ; woman's, premenstrual, **UB** 26, 28
Belladonna, cosmetic, **DL** 42
Belt, macrame, **CF** 108-114 ; for sundress, **SE** 110
Belting, curved, for skirt, **SE** 44
Benefit period, definition. **YM** 138
Berk, Lotte, on exercise, **UB** 97
Berry stain, removal, **UT** 23
Bias, definition, **SE** 136
Bicarbonate of soda in cooking vegetables, **FL** 56
Bicycling, **DL** 105 ; **GT** 110
Bikeways, **GT** 112
Bird, Caroline, on women employees, **PY** 29, 90
Birds as pets, **UT** 14
Birth control. *See* Contraception
Bits, for hand drills, **FB** 28 ; masonry, **FB** 40
Black students, education guides, **FT** 133
Blackheads, **DL** 34
Blanching of vegetables, loss of vitamin C, **FL** 37
Blanket stitch, definition, **SE** 136
Blankets, buying tips, **YM** 73
Bleaching of hair, **DL** 36, 66
Bleeding, internal, **GF** 131 ; management of, **GF** 130 ; of radiators, **FB** 81 ; post-menopausal, **UB** 135
Blind, the, information, **FT** 140
Blinds, vertical, **HD** 136 ; window, **HD** 52
Blood, body content, **GF** 130 ; loss, dangers of, **GF** 130 ; pressure, high, and heart disease, **FL** 105 ; stain, removal, **UT** 22
Bloody Mary, mixing, **UT** 39
Blouse, doll's, **SE** 128 ; soft, **SE** 45, 142
Blue Book of Manufacturers, **FT** 40 ; **YM** 76
Blue chips, **YM** 125
Blue Cross hospital plan, **YM** 115
Blue Shield insurance, **YM** 115
B'nai B'rith job clinics, **PY** 55
Body ; and mind, interrelationship, **FT** 97 ; bath-time care of, **DL** 75 ; erotic areas, **SS** 66 ; exercises, **DL** 92-115 ; language, **TW** 20 ; lifts,

Body

69

Boiling over

cosmetic, **DL** 143; responses, creation of the brain, **UB** 40; shapes of woman, **FL** 83 (chart); fashion changes in, **DL** 8-9; **UB** 8-9; tissue, repair, **FL** 17
Boiling over of food, prevention, **UT** 7
Bolts, Molly, **FB** 38
Bond, definition, **YM** 123
Bone, lodged in cat's mouth, **UT** 13; size, in personal weight calculation, **FL** 81
Boning of midriff, for evening skirt, **SE** 74
Books, as room decoration, **HD** 119; removal tip, **UT** 56
Boredom, in the stress syndrome, **UB** 48; leading to delinquency, **FT** 46; of the housewife, **KS** 62
Borrowing for College, **YM** 132
Borrowing money, for vacation, **GT** 22
Bottle art, **CF** 36-39
Bottle gardens, **UT** 55
Bottles, lamps from, **HD** 120
"Bowling alley" living room, decoration, **HD** 130
Boxes, decoupage, **CF** 103; storage, **HD** 74, 106
Boy(s) See also Childhood; puberty in, **GF** 43; young, conditioning of, toward girls, **WM** 46
Bra styles, and purposes for, **DL** 120-121; **UB** 143
Brackets, for shelving, **FB** 40
Brads, **FB** 33
Braille, publications in, **FT** 140
Brain, effect on, of excessive alcohol, **UB** 89; effect on rest of the body, **UB** 35, 37 (diagram); in sexual excitement, **UB** 38; in sleep, **UB** 40-41; seat of the senses, **UB** 37 (diagram), 38
Braking system, of car, **FB** 125
Brandy, in first aid, **GF** 141
Bread, calorie difference of wholemeal and white, **FL** 136; loss of vitamin B on toasting, **FL** 38; stale, use of, **UT** 7; wholegrain, **FL** 135
Breakdown of car, of the single woman, **OY** 143
Breakfast foods, **FL** 70
Breakfast time chaos in the family, **TW** 136
Break-in, precautions against, **OY** 141
Breast(s) cancer, detection, **UB** 140; cosmetic surgery for, **DL** 140-143; enlargement, cosmetic, **DL** 140; lump in, **UB** 140; reduction, cosmetic, **DL** 142; self examination of, in cancer screening, **UB** 118-119; uneven size, **UB** 140
Breastfeeding, and resumption of menstruation, **SS** 134; conception during, **SS** 95
Breathing, cessation of, first aid, **GF** 133; exercises, **UB** 110
Brief encounter, the, **SS** 81; **OY** 110
British Thermal Unit, **YM** 70
Broadloom carpeting, **HD** 42
Brocade skirt, **SE** 71
Brochure, for marketing of crafts **CF** 139
Broken love affair, the, **OY** 115
Broker, definition, **YM** 125
Bronzers, **DL** 32
Brush, paint, for home decoration, **HD** 33
Brushing of hair, **DL** 56, 58
Buckwheat, **FL** 136
Budget flying, **GT** 91
Budgeting, **YM** 18; during husband's unemployment, **FT** 40; for vacations, **GT** 21; of average American city worker, **YM** 21
"Building" characteristic, of the single woman, **OY** 78
Bullet wound, **GF** 131
Bunk beds, **HD** 22, 114
Bureau of Sport Fisheries and Wildlife, **GT** 112
Burglar in the house, what to do, **OY** 142
Burglary, car, **GT** 35; deterrent methods, **UT** 61
Burlap, **HD** 36, 49
Burned food, **UT** 7
Burns, first aid, **GF** 137; in wooden surface, repair, **UT** 21; ointments, **GF** 138
Bus tours, **GT** 96
Business, cards, for marketing of crafts, **CF** 139; jobs available in, **OY** 49; small, **FT** 133; **PY** 56
Bustline, exercises for, **DL** 94-95; **UB** 105
Butter, tips on buying and using, **YM** 32
Buttocks, cosmetic lift, **DL** 143
Buttoned cushion, **SE** 120
Buttons, dental floss anchorage, **UT** 60
Buying Guide, Consumer Reports, **YM** 56
Buying, jobs available in, **OY** 49; **PY** 140

Buying

Caesarian section

Camps

Caesarian section, repeated, **SS** 136
Cafe curtains, **HD** 136
Caffeine, **UB** 81
Cake, stale, reuse, **UT** 7
Calcium, dietary, **FL** 18 ; in good nutrition, **UB** 63
Calisthenics, **DL** 110
Calories, consumption, and overweight, **DL** 87 ; definition, **UB** 71 ; expenditure, and activity, **DL** 88 ; and overweight, **FL** 82 ; average, **UB** 72 ; in sexual intercourse, **SS** 132 ; normal, **FL** 85 ; food values, **GF** 63 (chart) ; requirements, of adolescents, **FL** 22, 23 ; of adults, **FL** 26, 27 ; of children, **FL** 18, 19, 22, 23
Calves, exercises for, **DL** 112-113
Campgrounds, guides, **GT** 46 ; improved, **GT** 44 ; private, **GT** 43 ; unimproved, **GT** 44
Camps and Camping, authorities offering facilities, **GT** 44 ; clubs, **GT** 46 ; first-time, preparation for, **GT** 42
Camps, for children, **PY** 122 ; safety rules, **GT** 46 ; site,

Camping vacations

choosing, **GT** 42
Camping vacations, **GT** 36, 42
Camping and Trailering Guide, **GT** 46
Camping in the National Park System, **GT** 45
Cancer, breast, detection, **UB** 140; incidence in women, **UB** 114; risk in breast cosmetic surgery, **DL** 141; sex distribution according to part affected, **UB** 116 (diagram); susceptibility of various parts of the body, **UB** 116 (diagram); warning signals, **UB** 116
Candle(s) decorative, **CF** 11; foils, **CF** 127, 135; hand-shaped, **CF** 53; making, **CF** 48-55; marketing of, **CF** 138; molded, **CF** 49-52, 55
Candlelight in the dining room, **HD** 80
Candlesticks, **UT** 32, 58
Cannabis, **FT** 73 (table)
Canned goods, tips on buying and using, **YM** 33
Canoeing, **GT** 66
Capabilities, unused, of woman, **KS** 30
Carbohydrates, **FL** 22; in diabetes, **FL** 108; in good nutrition, **UB** 64; in reducing diets, **DL** 84; **FL** 90, 93; **UB** 78
Career. *See also* Jobs; Occupations
Career, advice on, **PY** 54; days, college, **PY** 55; for the single woman. *See* Occupations, for the single woman; plans, discussion with employer, **PY** 87; prospective, for the teenager, **TW** 120; training, company subsidy for, **PY** 86
Carpet beetles, control of, **FB** 135
Carpets and carpeting; buying of, **HD** 42; **YM** 63; cigarette burn, repair, **UT** 59; construction, **HD** 43; disguise of glaring color, **HD** 135; fibers, **HD** 45 (table); measuring for, **HD** 42; textures, **HD** 44; tiles, **HD** 136
Carrots, mulching, **UT** 52
Carryall, beach, **SE** 33
Cars. *See* Automobiles
Case for the Working Mother, The, **PY** 126
Cash, raising of credit, **YM** 50
Casing, definition, **SE** 136
Cat repellents, **UT** 14

Cats, as pets, **UT** 12
Caulking, **FB** 86
Cedar chest, renovation, **UT** 59
Ceiling, lowering effect, **HD** 36
Celiac disease, diet for, **FL** 130
Cellulite, **DL** 75
Cements, fixit-job, **FB** 39; tile, **FB** 105
Center front (or back), definition, **SE** 136
Centerpiece in table decoration, **UT** 32
Ceramic tiles, **HD** 36; **FB** 105
Cereal grains, **FL** 136
Cereals, tips on buying and using, **YM** 33
Certified Public Accountant, **PY** 132
Cervical smear test, **UB** 119
Cervix, of the womb, **UB** 20
Cesspool, maintenance, **FB** 137; periodic inspection, **FB** 133
Chair, cushion, **SE** 113; rungs, repair, **UT** 18
Challenge, antidote to boredom, **KS** 66; in the search for happiness, **KS** 120; necessity for, in adolescence, **FT** 46
Chambers of Commerce, as information centers for vacations, **GT** 28, 31
Chameleons, as pets, **UT** 17
Champagne, **UT** 37; cocktail, **UT** 39; punch, **UT** 40
Chancre, **SS** 140
Change(s), accompanying ceremonies, **KS** 102; anticipation of, **KS** 92; as part of the natural order, **KS** 90; capacity for, **OY** 120; coping with, **KS** 89; of life. *See* Menopause; precursor of stress, units system, **FT** 101
Changing of tire, **FB** 122
Chartered Life Underwriter, **PY** 133
Chartered Property Casualty Underwriter, **PY** 133
Chastity, **SS** 18, 70
Checking accounts, **YM** 21
Checks, cost of, **YM** 22; types, **YM** 11
Checkup, health, for husbands, **GF** 55
Cheese, board, decoupage, **CF** 103; cooking ways, **FL** 48; economy tips, **UT** 7; nutrients in, **FL** 22; tips on buying and using, **YM** 32; varieties, **FL** 139
Chemical burns, first aid, **GF** 138
Chemopeel, **DL** 139

Chewing difficulties

Chewing difficulties in the

Chewing Gum

elderly, diet for, **FL** 132
Chewing Gum, removal, **UT** 22
Chicken, economic cooking of, **YM** 28
Children *See also* Adolescence; accidental poisoning in, **GF** 139; **HD** 94; accidents, **GF** 88, 136; adoption by parent's remarriage partner, **OY** 123; AFDC benefits for, **OY** 137; amusement of, on long journeys, **GT** 137; and courtship of parent, **OY** 113; and grandparents, **GF** 80; and remarriage of parent, **OY** 122; battered, **FT** 141; blind, advice and information, **FT** 140; camps, **PY** 122; car travel with, **GT** 26; care of, community facilities, **OY** 66; day centers, **PY** 118; in the one-parent family, **OY** 59; jobs available in, **OY** 48; of working mothers, **PY** 113; shared, of working couple, **PY** 108; claim for, as dependents, **OY** 134; communication with parents, **FT** 18; creative instinct in, **CF** 8; daily calorie requirements, **FL** 18, 19, 22, 23; deaf, parents' reading list, **FT** 140; development, from two to five years, **TW** 54-55 (chart); diabetic, **FT** 139; diet for good health, **GF** 25, 28 (table); disciplining, **OY** 133; **WM** 136; eating difficulties, **GF** 29; effect on, of mother's working, in the single-parent home, **OY** 59; enforced absence of father, **OY** 133; entertainment, on long car trips, **GT** 34; entry into school, **TW** 64; etiquette, **UT** 47; flexibility, in one-parent family, **OY** 38; freedom of, in one-parent family, **OY** 36; grandparents and, **GF** 80; growth rates, **FL** 26; **GF** 25; healthy, **GF** 25; height table, **GF** 27; help in the house, **OY** 74; **PY** 105; **TW** 137; hospitalization, **TW** 131; immunization schedule, **GF** 34; in competition with father, for mother's attention, **WM** 121; in the adult world, 12-13; individuality, **FT** 21; **GF** 20; **TW** 24; initiation into preschool center, **OY** 68; jealousy of each other, **FT** 23; "latchkey", **OY** 62; learning, **TW** 10-11; listening to, **TW** 17; lonely one, **TW** 87; masturbation in, **SS** 138; medical checkups, **GF** 34-35, 37; medical costs, divorced parent's responsibility for, **OY** 135; natural happiness of, **KS** 126; neglect of, by ambitious father, 64; obesity in, **GF** 30; obscene language in, **UT** 47; of alcoholic parents, **FT** 92; of divorced parents, divided loyalties, **OY** 36; of working mothers, **PY** 14-15, 111; chores for, **PY** 105; independence, **PY** 126; on vacation, **GT** 18, 26, 137; overprotected, of the newly single parent, **OY** 35; party, **UT** 44; prodigies, **TW** 12-13; reaction to loss of parent, **OY** 34; relationship with working mother, **OY** 60; retarded, help for parents, **FT** 141; room, arrangement, **HD** 114; decorating ideas, **HD** 20; floor coverings, **HD** 39; lighting, **HD** 82; school age, early morning lethargy in, **TW** 136; self-esteem in, **TW** 25; sexual feeling in, **SS** 138; sick, **GF** 105; amusement of, **GF** 122 (table), 116; examination of, **GF** 110-111; sick, meals for, **FL** 131; of the working mother, **OY** 69; **PY** 122; single-parent, **OY** 29; sleep requirements, **GF** 32, 35; stress in, **FT** 110; **GF** 110; teeth, **GF** 36, 38; temporary separation from parent, **TW** 130; through the ages, **TW** 6-7; upbringing of, father's role in, **WM** 122; weight table, **GF** 27; world of, **TW** 14-15; young, attachment to parent of opposite sex, **TW** 56; awkward questions, how to answer them, **TW** 49; development patterns, **TW** 36-37; discipline of, **TW** 38; independence in, **TW** 43; punishment, **TW** 40; rebellion in, **TW** 42
Child Sense, William Homan, **GF** 29
Childbearing in former years, **SS** 86

Childbirth

Childbirth, as sexual climax, **SS** 52; pregnancy following,

73

Childhood

SS 135
Childhood, fears of, **TW** 130; illnesses, **GF** 106 (table); separation of the sexes in, **WM** 48-49
Childish behavior, in man, **WM** 87
Childlessness, **SS** 52
Children's Bureau, Department of Health, Education and Welfare, **FT** 140
Children's librarian, work of, **PY** 130
Child-teacher relationship, **TW** 70
Chilling of drinks, **UT** 36
Chimneys, periodic inspection, **FB** 133
Chin, cosmetic surgery, **DL** 134
Chinagraph pencil, **CF** 81
Chinese, money usage, **YM** 9
Chiropodist, regular visits to, **UB** 124
Chlortetracycline food dip, **FL** 41
Chocolate stain, removal, **UT** 22
Choker, bead, **CF** 30
Choking, accidental, in babies, **GF** 90
Cholesterol, **FL** 100, 101, 106; **GF** 58
Chores of the house, children's share in, **OY** 74; **PY** 105; **TW** 137, 138
Christening gown, **SE** 61
Christian church, attitude to sex, **SS** 27
Christmas decorations, **CF** 126-36
Christopher D. Smithers Foundation, **FT** 92
Chuck, of electric drill, **FB** 28
Cigarette burn in carpet, repair, **UT** 59; smoking, effect on complexion, **DL** 32
Circuit breakers, **FB** 59
Circular curtaining, **HD** 100
Circumcision, **UB** 143
Circus party, **UT** 46
Cirrhosis of the liver, **UB** 89
City life, **OY** 81; **UB** 11
Civil service jobs for women, **PY** 66
Clamp(s), **FB** 48, 49
Clark, Linda, on health and beauty, **UB** 94
Clay pots, **UT** 53
Cleaning the home, **HD** 94
Cleansing liquid, brush application, **DL** 35; of skin, **DL** 28
Clergy Consultation Service on Abortion, **FT** 57, 135
Clippings, plastic mounting, **UT** 59
Clitoris, **SS** 58, 132; **UB** 18
Clogged drains, remedy for, **FB** 54; sinks, remedy for, **FB** 54, 55; toilet bowl, remedy for, **FB** 56
Closet auger, **FB** 57
Cloth, pressing, for home sewing, **SE** 24; texture, in fashion buying, **DL** 124
Clothes, buying tips, **DL** 120; **YM** 36, 41-43; consciousness through the ages, **SE** 8-9; do's and don'ts of fashion, **DL** 122-123; fashions in, 117; for dolls, **SE** 125; labeling of, law on, **YM** 135; laundering according to label, **YM** 135; mass production, **SE** 16-17; moths, control of, **FB** 135; refashioning of, **DL** 118-119; skiing, **GT** 75; teenage, symbol of independence, **TW** 105
Club, camping, **GT** 46; instinct, in man, **WM** 88; outdoor, **GT** 77
Coat, baby's, **SE** 65
Cocaine abuse, **FT** 71, 73 (table), 74
Cockroaches, control of, **FB** 135
Coffee, harmful effects, **UB** 81, 83; party, **UT** 29; stain, removal, **UT** 22
Coffee table, in mosaic, **CF** 18-23; of motifs in clear plastic, **CF** 62
Coins, ancient, **YM** 9
Coitus interruptus, **SS** 98
Cola, addictive property, **UB** 10
Collagen thickness of the skin, **FL** 121
Collars, bead, **CF** 30-31
Collector's table, **HD** 108
College, community two-year, **PY** 130; education, financing of, advice on, **YM** 132; entry rate, **YM** 130; junior, or state university? **YM** 130
Color, and light, interaction, **HD** 77; chart, for fashion buying, **DL** 125; in buying clothes, **DL** 120-121; in fashion buying, **DL** 124; in floor coverings, **HD** 39; in home decorating, **HD** 19; in wall decoration, **HD** 26; of food, **FL** 41
Colorants, food, **FL** 41, 140
Coma position, **GF** 141
Comb, heated, in hair straightening, **DL** 63; medieval, **DL** 12
Combination square, **FB** 28, 31

Combination square

Comfort

Comfort, in the home, **HD** 22, 87, 93
Commercial art, career prospects, in, **PY** 142
Commitment, in the love affair, **SS** 84
Communication, baby's first attempts, **TW** 33; distortion by parent, **TW** 30; in marriage, **SS** 57; **WM** 130; parent-child, **TW** 17, 136; parent-teenager, **FT** 78; **TW** 102; wife-husband, **KS** 48; within the family, **FT** 17
Community, college, two-year, **PY** 130; part in, of the single woman, **OY** 124; services for the elderly, **GF** 78; spirit, and safety of the single woman, **OY** 142; work, antidote to boredom, **KS** 73
Community Mental Health Centers, **FT** 142
Companionship in marriage, **SS** 57
Competence of woman, **FB** 14-15
Competition, in school life, **TW** 74; neighborly, **KS** 106, 108; nurtured by advertising, **KS** 108
Competitiveness in friendship, **WM** 78, 80; of the man's world, **WM** 62
Complaining, persistent, **KS** 140
Complaint against discrimination, procedure, **PY** 94
Complexion, **DL** 28
Compliance review, **PY** 90
Compounding of interest rates, **YM** 23
Computer programming, for women, **PY** 132
Concealer, cosmetic, **DL** 49
Conception, during breast-feeding period, **SS** 95; during menstruation, **SS** 132; following miscarriage, **SS** 135; reduced chance of, with very frequent intercourse, **SS** 137
Concussion, first aid, **GF** 136
Condom, **SS** 96, 143
Condominium living, **YM** 90-91
Confidante, in marriage, **KS** 143
Confidence, in reducing diets, **FL** 126
Confidences, interfamily, **KS** 143
Conflict, in marriage, **WM** 131
Conformism, social, **KS** 114
Connoisseur, **GT** 30
Consistency, in child rearing, **TW** 40

Constipation, **UB** 87
Consumer Reports, **YM** 56, 64
Consumer Reports Buying Guide, **YM** 76
Consumer Swindlers and How to Avoid Them, **YM** 140
Consumer's Guide to Better Buying, **YM** 35, 54
Contact, physical, in babyhood, **TW** 28
Containers, flower, for table decoration, **UT** 32; for pot plants, **HD** 102
Continuing Education Programs and Services for Women, **PY** 56
Continuity thread in life, **PY** 50
Contentment, **KS** 118
Continental Trailways discount passes, **GT** 100
Contouring, in make-up, **DL** 46, 47
Contraception, **SS** 86; advice to the teenager, **TW** 139; effecting wife's freedom, **SS** 86, 89; methods, **SS** 96-97 (table)
Contraceptive, pill, **SS** 89; and double standard of sexual behavior, **SS** 23; ethics of, **SS** 20; in relief of premenstrual symptoms, **UB** 28, 32; resumption after childbirth, **SS** 135; side effects, **SS** 90; **UB** 142
Contraceptive propaganda, **SS** 92, 93
Contract, mortgage, **YM** 100; of credit, **YM** 49, 50
Contrast, in home decorating, **HD** 26, 42
Convalescence, of the sick child, **GF** 116
Convenience foods, **FL** 32; **YM** 34
Conversation, art of, **KS** 137
Cooking, **FL** 47; camping equipment, **GT** 40; destruction of vitamins, **FL** 37; fire precautions, **HD** 94; for the diabetic, **FL** 108; for dieters, **DL** 88; ranges, buying of, **YM** 69; through the ages, **FL** 14-15
Cooling system, of car, **FB** 124
Co-operative apartment living, **YM** 91
Co-operative shopping, **YM** 36
"Coping" characteristic, of the single woman, **OY** 78
Cord, electric, repair of, **FB** 63; switch on, **FB** 66; lamp, replacement, **FB** 65
Cording, **SE** 121, 136

Cording

75

Corduroy

Corduroy, for girl's jumper, **SE** 37
Cork, wall covering, **HD** 36
Corner, mitering, **SE** 80, 82, 92, 94; rollers, **HD** 34
Cornflakes, **FL** 38, 70
Coronary thrombosis, **FL** 100
Corseting, of 1919, **UB** 9
Cosmetic stain, removal, **UT** 23
Cosmetic surgery, **DL** 129; cost, **DL** 132, first procedures, **DL** 131; historical background, **DL** 130; motivation for, **DL** 131; of arms, **DL** 143; of breasts, **DL** 140-143; of buttocks, **DL** 143; of chin, **DL** 134; of ears, **DL** 135; of face, *See* Facelifts; of jaw, **DL** 134; of nose, **DL** 128, 132; of stomach, **DL** 143; of thighs, **DL** 143
Cosmetics, **DL** 41; allergenic, **DL** 50; as aid to healthy looks, **FL** 124; hypoallergenic, **DL** 50; "natural", **UT** 60; pricing factor, **DL** 52; psychology factor, **FL** 126
Cotton, Dorothy Whyte, on the working mother, **PY** 126
Could Your Child Become an Alcoholic? **FT** 132
Council on International Educational Exchange, **GT** 89
Counseling, job opportunities in, **PY** 131-132
Counter space, emergency, in the kitchen, **UT** 7
Countersink, for hand drill, **FB** 28
Countersinking of nailheads, **FB** 35; of screwheads, **FB** 36, 37
Country music, Opryland, Nashville, **GT** 116
"Couple-oriented" society, and the newly single woman, **OY** 92
Court proceedings, juvenile, secrecy, **FT** 131
Cow, cure of whooping cough, **UB** 12
Cowboy placemats, **SE** 52
Cracks, wall, repairs, **FB** 101
Craft Shops/Galleries, USA, **GT** 29
Crafts, as art, **CF** 14; front-porch selling of, **CF** 142; encouraging child's learning, **TW** 73; marketing of, **CF** 138; in department stores, **CF** 141; materials, suppliers for, **CF** 142; of 400 years ago, **CF** 8; tax payable on money earned from, **CF** 142; vacations, **GT** 80
Crash diets, **DL** 84; **FL** 137
Crawl space, periodic inspection, **FB** 133
Crease-resistance, in fabric for home sewing, **SE** 26
Creation, need for, **CF** 8-9
Creche, paper, **CF** 128-131
Credit, buying, **YM** 45; contract, **YM** 49, 50; main uses for, **YM** 48 (chart); proportional use of in American families, **YM** 47 (chart); cards, **YM** 51; law on, **YM** 53; status, determining factors, **OY** 138; unions, **YM** 22
Crib, baby's slat regulations, **UT** 61
Crises, in development of personality, **OY** 23; family, through the ages, **FT** 6-7
Crochet decorations in the home, **HD** 125
Cronin, Tom, **DL** 141
Cross-country skiing, **GT** 75
Crosscut saw, **FB** 26
Crosswise-of-grain, definition, **SE** 136
Cruising vacations, **GT** 98; windjammer, **GT** 65
Crying, of babies, as means of communication, **TW** 26
"Cup-handle" ears, **DL** 135
Curtains and curtaining, **HD** 49, 55, 100; buying tips, **HD** 56; labeling of, **YM** 136; macrame, **CF** 115; sheer, **HD** 57; shower, **HD** 133
Curving of belting, **SE** 44
Cushion chair, **SE** 113
Cushions, **HD** 138; **SE** 118
Customs clearance, abroad, **GT** 141; U.S., **GT** 140
Cut, first aid for, **GF** 131
Cynicism, and the search for happiness, **KS** 126

Cystitis

Cystitis, **UB** 138

D and C

Death

D and C., **UB** 141
Daily Food Guide, U.S. Department of Agriculture, **FL** 141
Daiquiri, mixing, **UT** 39
Dancing, health value of, **UB** 97
Danger signals of ill health, **GF** 86
Dart, definition, **SE** 136
Data Processing Management Association, **PY** 133
Dating, for the single woman, **OY** 108; before remarriage, **OY** 121
Daughter, of the working mother, **PY** 126
Davis, Adelle, on nutrition, **UB** 62
Day care centers. *See under* Child, care of
Day in the life of a housewife, **UB** 44-45
Deaf child, the, parents' reading list, **FT** 140
Death, child's fear of, **TW** 133; child's questions on, **TW** 56, 133; fear of, **GF** 82; close, explanation to child, **TW** 133; the ultimate stress, **FT** 102; of parent, explanation to child, **OY** 29, 32; reaction of child,

77

Debt

Debt, OY 34
Debt, 1972 American, for installment buying, YM 50 (chart); load, criteria for, YM 47
Decision making, for the single woman, OY 26, 76; of the mature woman, KS 28
Decorating, home, accessories, HD 87; doors, HD 96; personal philosophy, HD 18; tricks and transformations, HD 132
Decoupage, CF 94-103; marketing of, CF 139; technique, CF 98
Deep freezers. *See* Freezer
Defensive behavior, of the newly single woman, OY 92
Defrosting techniques, UT 59
Delicacies, food, FL 10-11
Delinquency, minor, of the adolescent, FT 45
Delivery, estimation of date, SS 136
Denial, in anxiety, KS 140
Denim, barbecue apron, SE 101; placemats, SE 52; storage man, HD 113; trouser making, SE 96
Dental, floss, anchorage of buttons, UT 60; health, FL 123; hygiene, training in, PY 136; insurance, YM 116
Dentition of children, GF 36, 38
Deodorants, DL 76; UB 125; mouth, UB 121; vaginal, UB 126
Department of Agriculture, food, inspection, FL 43
Department stores, in marketing of crafts, CF 141
Dependency, KS 133
Dependents, in divorce finance, OY 134
Depilatories, DL 36, 74-77
Depressant drugs, GF 50 (table), 72 (table)
Depression, effect on sex life, SS 106; following miscarriage, SS 136; incidence, FT 113; permanent, KS 132
Dermabrasion, DL 138
Dermatologists qualified to perform cosmetic surgery, DL 131
Detection of disease, early, UB 114
Development of the child, from two to five years, TW 54-55 (chart); from birth to 18 months, TW 36-37; slow, in puberty, TW 139; personal, in search for happiness, KS 119
Diabetes, FL 107; diet in, FL 132, 133; in children, advice and information, FT 139
Diaphragm, contraceptive, SS 91
Diarrhea, Montezuma's Revenge, GT 134
Diet, DL 83; 1000 Calorie, FL 85, 86; 1200 Calorie, FL 88; 1500 Calorie, FL 88; and facelifts, DL 136; balanced, FL 18; UB 61, 64, 70; crash, dangers, FL 137; daily family, official guide FL 141; fattening, DL 91; FL 94; for celiac disease, FL 130; for health reasons, FL 96; for healthy hair, DL 57; for peptic ulcer, FL 131; for the too-thin, DL 91; FL 94; in adolescence, GF 45; in constipation, UB 87; in diabetes, FL 132, 133; in fever conditions, FL 131; in ill health, FL 130; in premenstrual time, UB 28; in treatment of acne, GF 45; low-carbohydrate, FL 93; low-cholesterol, FL 102; low-residue, FL 130; macrobiotic, FL 77; minimum daily requirements, UB 66-67 (table); of the sick child, GF 113; salt-restricted, FL 105; reducing, FL 85 et seq., 137, UB 77; for children, GF 32; for husbands, GF 56
Dietician, work of, PY 136
Digestive disorders, induced by emotional stress, UB 43
Digs, archeological, GT 86
Dimmer switches, HD 82
Dining Room, curtained-off, HD 100; floor coverings, HD 40; instant, HD 100; lighting, HD 79, 132
Dipping method, of candle making, CF 53
Directory of Agencies Serving the Visually Handicapped in the United States, FT 140
Directory of Approved Counseling Agencies, PY 54
Directory of Vocational Counseling Services, OY 47
Discipline, of children, TW 38; as part of love for them, GF 18; of single parent, OY 60, 133; of working mothers, PY 117
Discontentment, of the wife, KS 140
Discount buying, UT 6; of household appliances, YM 70
Discrimination against women,

Discrimination against women

Discrimination in friendship

in employment, **PY** 74, 90
Discrimination in friendship, for the single woman, **OY** 94
Discussion, within the family, **FT** 27
Dishes, buying tips, **YM** 72
Dishwashers, buying of, **YM** 68
Diskin, Eve, **DL** 108
Distemper **UT** 10
Divorce, **KS** 100; age factor, **FT** 116; child's reaction, **OY** 34; explanation to children, **OY** 29, 31; father's visiting rights, **OY** 36; financial arrangements, **OY** 134; incidence, **FT** 115; procedure, **FT** 137; remarriage after, **FT** 126; **OY** 121; incidence, **OY** 119 (chart); sexual difficulties, **SS** 80, 82
Divorced, the man, incidence, **OY** 22 (chart); woman, **OY** 10, 17; earnings, and assessment for welfare benefit, **OY** 137; financial problems, **OY** 134; incidence, **OY** 22 (chart); sense of purpose, **OY** 20, 42
DMT, **FT** 68
Dogs as pets, **UT** 11
Do-it-yourself, hazards of, **GF** 98
Doctor, child's fear of, **TW** 131; family, through the ages, **GF** 8-9; on vacation abroad, **GT** 135; when to call, **GF** 105, 108
Dog, car traveling with, **GT** 34
Doll party, **UT** 45
Dollar, declining purchasing power of, **YM** 19
Doll's clothes, **SE** 125
Domination of woman, by family, **KS** 108
Doorbell, replacement, **FB** 70
"Doormat" of the family, **KS** 46
Doors, decorative, **HD** 96; non-closing, **FB** 91, 92; periodic inspection, **FB** 133; sticking, **FB** 89; weatherstripping, **FB** 85
Door-to-door callers, and the single woman, **OY** 141
Double life of woman, **KS** 28
Double chin, cosmetic surgery for, **DL** 134
Douching, **SS** 143; **UB** 126
Downspouts, periodic inspection, **FB** 133
Draft control in the home, **FB** 84
Drains, **FB** 54, 133
Draperies, **HD** 55; buying tips, **HD** 56; for picture windows, **HD** 49; for traditional windows, **HD** 52
Drawers, sticking, **UT** 18
Dreams, **TW** 62; **UB** 132
Dress, baby's, **SE** 69; batik-dyed, **CF** 79; dye-painted, **CF** 67; from soft blouse pattern, **SE** 142; halter-neck, **SE** 84
Dressing and undressing, in arousing husband's excitement, **SS** 64-65
Drilling holes, in wood, **FB** 34; masonry, **FB** 40, 41; technique, **FB** 29; tools for the handywoman, **FB** 28
Drills, for the handywoman, **FB** 28, 30
Drinking, excessive, gauge of, **UB** 86; for dieters, **DL** 89; water abroad, **GT** 134
Drinks, alcoholic, calorie values, **GF** 64-65; mixing, **UT** 38; useful tips, **UT** 36
Dripping faucets, **FB** 49; **UT** 56
Dripping, meat, **UT** 9
Drive system, of car, **FB** 124
Driving alone, safety precautions, **OY** 143; night, **FB** 126; reckless, of teenagers, **FT** 131; tips, **FB** 126, 127
Dropouts, teenage, **FT** 52
Drug abuse, **FT** 12-13, 63, 72-73 (table); community research groups, **FT** 75; extra-family help, **FT** 78; helping agencies, **FT** 132; in adolescence, **GF** 49; in the teenager, **FT** 77; **TW** 112, 142; in women, **UB** 91, 92; need for parents' information on, **FT** 74; opportunities for, **FT** 77; common names for, **FT** 72-73 (table); signs of, in your child, **FT** 69, 75
Drugs, **GF** 50-51 (table); as aid to reducing diets, **FL** 138; cost of, generic-proprietary differential, **YM** 139; generic name, **YM** 139; information on, to teenagers, **TW** 142; overdose, treatment of unconsciousness, **GF** 140
Drugs. Parents and Children, Rosenthal and Mothner, **GF** 50
Dry complexion, care of, **DL** 30
Dry rot, control of, **FB** 136
Dubonnet cocktail, **UT** 39
Duty items, abroad, **GT** 141
Dye Bazaar, Marrakech, **YM** 14
Dye-painting of clothes, **CF** 64-67

Dye painting

79

Early marriage

Ejaculation

Early marriage, **SS** 76
Ears, correction of, **DL** 135
Earthquake, **FB** 131
Ease, definition, **SE** 136
Eating, habits, **FL** 118; **UB** 75
Eating, social significance, **UB** 75
Economy, in home decorating, **HD** 23
Edges, finish of, **SE** 136
Education, for black students, guides, **FT** 133; for the blind child, **FT** 140; further, **PY** 56; **YM** 130; planning for, **YM** 130; vacations, **GT** 79
Educational Expeditions

International, **GT** 89
Educational Vacations, **GT** 81
Eggs, buying and using tips, **UT** 7; **YM** 32; cooking ways, **FL** 48; in cosmetics, **FL** 126; in hair care, **DL** 58; ovary content, **UB** 143
Eggshell, for cleaning narrow-necked vessels, **UT** 59; painting, **CF** 16
Ego, man's, and his working wife, **PY** 103
Ejaculation, extra-vaginal, causing pregnancy, **SS** 132; first, **GF** 43

Elderly

Elderly, the, accidents at home, **GF** 96; care of, **GF** 72; community, **GF** 78; chewing difficulties, diet in, **FL** 132; companionship for, **GF** 82; indigestion, diet for, **FL** 132; nutritional requirements, **GF** 86; **FL** 29; signs of illness in, **GF** 86
Electric shock, **FB** 73; treatment, **GF** 141
Electrical appliances, checking before repair, **FB** 72; maintenance, **FB** 137
Electrical equipment, of home furnace, **FB** 79
Electrical repairs for the handywoman, **FB** 58; rules for, **FB** 59
Electrical system, of car, **FB** 124
Electrician's pliers, **FB** 26
Electricity in the home, dangers, **GF** 100; insulation, **UT** 60
Electrolysis, **DL** 36
Emancipation, sexual, of woman, **SS** 17
Emasculating woman, the, **KS** 57
Emergency, accident, **GF** 100
Emotions. *See also* Stress; and the menstrual cycle **UB** 16; of the woman left single, **OY** 22; outward signs, **UB** 39
Employment. *See also* Occupation; agency, commercial, **PY** 65; for the single woman, **OY** 53; state, **PY** 66; etiquette, **PY** 89; policy, statement, **PY** 93
Emulsifiers, food additives, **FL** 41
Enamel work, **CF** 80-85
Encouragement, of children, **TW** 42, 74
Endocrine glands, **UB** 26
Endometrium, **UB** 20
Endowment policy, for education, **YM** 131
Energy balance, in perfect body weight, **FL** 82; expenditure, and calorie consumption, **GF** 63 (table)
Energy-giving foods, **UB** 64
Enjoying your toddler, **TW** 47
Entertaining, hints on, **UT** 25; in the home, **HD** 92; for the single woman, **OY** 100
Envy, encouraged by advertising, **KS** 106
Enzymes, **UB** 63
Eosin, **DL** 50
Epilepsy, information, **FT** 139
Epoxy patching compound, **FB** 47, 49
Equal Employment Opportunity Act of 1972, **PY** 91, 92
Equal Employment Opportunity Commission, **PY** 92, 93
Equal Pay Act of 1963, **PY** 91, 92
Erection, **SS** 66
Escalator clause, of separation agreement, **OY** 134
Essential fatty acids, **FL** 22
Esteem, mutual, in premarital lovemaking, **SS** 77
Estrogen, **UB** 23
Etiquette, children's, **UT** 47
Eurail pass, **GT** 100
Eurobus passes, **GT** 101
Europe, vacation accommodation, **GT** 102; vacation travel in, **GT** 100
Evening gown, doll's, **SE** 135
Evening out for the single woman, personal safety precautions, **OY** 142
"Everything" box, **HD** 106
Examination, medical, routine, **UB** 116
Excitement, brain-body relationship in, **UB** 41
Exercise(s), **DL** 92-115; and dieting, **DL** 88; and reducing, **FL** 90; **GF** 60; **UB** 78; breathing, **UB** 110; calorie values, **GF** 63 (table); recommended for women, **UB** 102; embarking on a campaign, **DL** 114; for health, **UB** 94; for the busy mother, **GF** 120; for the elderly, **GF** 84; for women, **UB** 102-109; in adolescence, **GF** 46-47; in pregnancy, **SS** 137; in working off anger, **UB** 56; individual needs for, **DL** 104; isometric, **UB** 100; relationship with mental alertness, **KS** 73; relaxation, **UB** 55; within daily routine, **UB** 109; yoga, **UB** 99
Exhaust system, of car, **FB** 126
Exhibition, outdoor, **CF** 17
Expansion-type anchors, **FB** 38; screws, **FB** 38, 39
Expression of feelings, **TW** 22; **UB** 56
Extra-marital love affair, as temporary escape, **SS** 80
"Extraordinary medical costs" of children, parent's responsibility for, **OY** 135
Eyebrows, **DL** 36, 47
Eyelifts, **DL** 137; length of hospitalization, **DL** 138; risks of, **DL** 138; scarring, **DL** 138

Eyes

Eyes, make-up, **DL** 47-49; regular examination of, **UB** 121; routine care of, **UB** 121

Fabric

Fake fur bedspread

Fabric, curtain, **HD** 56; **YM** 136; correct needle for, **SE** 24; grain, **SE** 136, 138, 139; in carpet buying, **YM** 63; in clothes buying, **YM** 38; nap (pile), definition, **SE** 138; protective sprays, **HD** 138; synthetic, buying tips, **YM** 43; thread count, **YM** 136; through the ages, **SE** 10-13; upholstery, buying tips, **UT** 59; variety of, for the home needlewoman, **SE** 24-25, 26; wall coverings, **HD** 36; widths, **SE** 26
Face, as others see it, **DL** 26; barometer of the body, **DL** 39; care of, need for regularity, **DL** 39; exercises, 38-39; hair on, **DL** 35; lines of, meanings, **KS** 84; mask, **DL** 36-37; of beauty, **DL** 6-7; rouge application, **DL** 47; shape, hairstyles for, **DL** 68-69
Facelifts, **DL** 136; cost, **DL** 138; operative procedure, **DL** 137
Facing, definition, **SE** 136
Facts of life, **SS** 139; **TW** 51
Failed love affair, **SS** 74
Fainting, treatment, **GF** 141
Fake fur bedspread, **SE** 77

Fallopian tubes

Fallopian tubes, **UB** 20; in female sterilization, **SS** 98; in gonorrhea, **SS** 142
Falls, first aid, **GF** 136
Family, the, **WM** 18-19. *See also* Marriage; arguments, **TW** 136; as reason for marriage, **WM** 108; budgeting, **YM** 18; caring for elderly members, **GF** 73; code of behavior, **FT** 27; crisis, **FT** 6-7, 60; definition, **GF** 6-7; discussion, **FT** 27; **TW** 97, 107; doctor, through the ages, **GF** 8-9; dovetailing of activities, **TW** 96; excursions, in encouraging learning, **TW** 73; favoritism among children, **FT** 22; finance, **FT** 121; **YM** 18; **OY** 133; hobbies, finding room for, **HD** 18; insurance in, **YM** 107; inter-relationship, **FT** 23; jealousy, **TW** 76; man's maturity within, **WM** 54-55; meals, Daily Food Guide, **FL** 141; model for average income and expenditure, **YM** 21; mutual support in, **FT** 14-15, 43; **GF** 22; occupational integration in, **WM** 67-68; of the successful man, **WM** 64; one-parent, **OY** 29; relationships, of the working mother, **PY** 124; rules, **FT** 27; sexual identity within, **WM** 36; social service agency, **OY** 67; stress in **FT** 97; preventive measures, **FT** 102; sources, **FT** 100; support, in teenage problems, **FT** 43; therapy, in stress, **FT** 100; through the ages, **GF** 6-7; troubles, outside advice, **FT** 24, 57, 59; preventive measures, **FT** 25; vacations, **GT** 17
Family Institute of New York City, **FT** 100
Family Planning Information Service, New York, **FT** 135
Family Service Association of America, **FT** 134, 137
Farm and Countryside Ranch Guide, **GT** 72
Farm vacations, **GT** 69
Fashion, **DL** 117; buying, career in, **PY** 140; model, **DL** 19
Fasteners for hollow walls, **FB** 37; for the handywoman, **FB** 33; masonry, **FB** 38, 40
Fastening jobs, tools for, **FB** 24
Fat(s), **FL** 22; and cholesterol level, **GF** 58; body, **FL** 81; dietary, and blood cholesterol level, **FL** 102; sources, **FL** 103 (chart); in diet of diabetics, **FL** 132, 133; in diet of the well-to-do, **FL** 96; in good nutrition, **UB** 64; in reducing diets, **FL** 91; **UB** 78
Father, ambitions for son, **WM** 60
Father, contact with small baby, **TW** 28; divorced, disappearance of, **OY** 37; visiting rights, **OY** 36; first relationship with daughter, **WM** 34; help with home duties, **GF** 123; in competition with children for wife's attention, **WM** 121; discipline of children, **WM** 136; in family life, **GF** 22-23; in relief of mother-baby tension, **TW** 30; in sex education of the very young child, **TW** 53; participation in child's upbringing, **WM** 122
Father figure, for the child of one-parent family, **OY** 38
Fatherless child, adaptability, **OY** 40
Fatigue, wifely, **KS** 61
Fattening diet, **DL** 91; **FL** 94
Fattest recorded man, **GF** 59
Fatty acids, **FL** 100, 102
Faucet, dismantling of, **FB** 49, 51; leaky, **FB** 49; **UT** 56; parts of, **FB** 50
Favoritism among children, **FT** 22
FDA. *See* Food and Drug Administration
Fear(s), brain-body relationship, **UB** 41; of childhood, **TW** 61, 130
Federal Careers for Women, **PY** 66
Federal Housing Authority, (FHA), **YM** 93
Federal jobs for women, **PY** 66
Fee(s), employment agency, **PY** 66; in child care, **PY** 118
Feeding infants on long journeys, **GT** 138
Feelings, expression of, **TW** 22; **UB** 56; intensity, in the young child, **TW** 60
Feet, Chinese binding of, **UB** 9; crippling by fashion, **UB** 9; routine care of, **UB** 124
Female Eunuch, The, **SS** 84
Femininity, definition, **KS** 54
Fertility, and vitamin E, **FL** 74; declining, **SS** 136
Feverish illness, diet for, **FL** 131
FHA loan for home remodeling, **YM** 103; mortgage, **YM** 100

FHA loan

Fiber glass

Fiber glass, **HD** 142; **UT** 21
Fibers, man-made, **HD** 139-143 (table)
Fibroid tumor, **UB** 141
Fidelity in marriage, **SS** 52, 55
Filters, heating system, **FB** 81
Finance(s), family, during unemployment, **FT** 40; of divorce, **FT** 137; **OY** 134; problems, of enforced separation of husband and wife, **OY** 133
Finger foods, serving technique, **UT** 31
Fingernails, mirror of health state, **FL** 122
Finish of edges, **SE** 136
Finishes, floor, **FB** 112
Fire in electrical appliance, **FB** 73; in the home, emergency procedures, **FB** 131; prevention, **HD** 94; insurance, **YM** 119
Fireplace in the bedroom, treatment, **HD** 133
First aid, **GF** 100, 102, 130; vacation kit, **GT** 135
Fish, as pets, **UT** 16; gift-wrapping, **CF** 126, 132; home filleting, **UT** 9; home storage, **FL** 63 (table); go-togethers, **FL** 142; mobile, **CF** 125; shopping for, **FL** 32
Fish House punch, **UT** 40
Fitness, and beauty, **UB** 94
Fitzgerald, Scott, to Ernest Hemingway, on the rich, **KS** 124
Fixit jobs, rules for, **FB** 18; tools for, **FB** 20; kit, for the handywoman, **FB** 21, 23
Flared skirt, **SE** 41
Flat tire, changing procedure, **FB** 122
Flat-bed sewing machine, **SE** 24
Flattery, in love, **WM** 98
Flavor loss, in food processing, **FL** 42
Flexibility, in dealing with the preteener, **TW** 95; in marriage, **FT** 118; of woman, **KS** 22, 96
Flirting, **WM** 38-43
Float trips, **GT** 67
Flood, precautionary measures, **FB** 131
Floors, covering, characterization of rooms, **HD** 41; hard-surface, **HD** 47; determining factors, **HD** 39; mobility factor, **HD** 41; finishers, **FB** 112; garden, **UT** 55; planning in home decorating, **HD** 39; squeaking, **FB** 114; tiles, resilient, **FB** 108; wooden, repair, **FB** 108
Flour, dusting technique, **UT** 17; wholegrain, **FL** 72, 135
Flowers, arrangements in the home, **HD** 89; arranging for pressing, **CF** 92-93; dried, **HD** 90; **UT** 35; in clear plastic, **CF** 56-63; picture, **CF** 95; pot containers, mosaic, **CF** 25; pressing, **CF** 90-95; stain, removal, **UT** 23
Flues, periodic inspection, **FB** 133
Fluid, body, premenstrual, **UB** 28; loss, in burns, **GF** 137
Flushing of toilet, insufficient, remedy for, **FB** 53
Fluted skirt, **SE** 49
Fly/cruise vacations, **GT** 96
Fly/drive tours, **GT** 94
Flying doctor service of Australia, **GF** 9
Foam pad, paint, **HD** 33
Fog, driving in, **FB** 126
Foil decorations, **CF** 134
Folk remedies, **GF** 10-11; **UB** 12-13
Follicle stimulating hormone (FSH), **UB** 23
Follower, how to deal with, **OY** 143
Food(s), additives, **FL** 39, 44 (table); flavor, **FL** 42; nutritional, **FL** 42; buying and using tips, **UT** 6; **YM** 27, 32-33; buying of, for the freezer, **YM** 66; calorie values, **GF** 63 (chart); child's requirements for health, **GF** 25, 28 (table); colorants, **FL** 41, 140; colors, **FL** 41; compensatory role of, **UB** 75; complementary wines, **UT** 41; components in cosmetics, **FL** 124; constituents, **UB** 70-71 (table); convenience, **FL** 32; **YM** 34; cosmetic value of, **DL** 90; cost of, effect of inflation, **YM** 29 (graphs); delicacies, **FL** 10-11; effect of pesticides, **FL** 44; equation with love, **GF** 30; for camping, **GT** 41; for health and beauty, **DL** 90; for the family, Daily Food Guide, **FL** 141; freezing at home, **FL** 62; function of **FL** 17; health, **FL** 67; high cholesterol, **FL** 106; high sodium, **FL** 109; in the psychology of love, **FL** 126; labeling, **FL** 36; leftovers,

Food(s)

Food and Drug Administration

storage, **UT** 6 ; main groups for good nutrition, **UB** 70 ; minimum daily requirements, **UB** 66-67 (table) ; not to freeze, **FL** 64 ; of pets, **UT** 10, 11, 13, 15, 16 ; of ritual, **FL** 8-9 ; official inspection, **FL** 43 ; organization, for the single working mother, **OY** 72 ; packaging, **FL** 33 ; party, **UT** 26, 28 ; perishable, home storage, **FL** 62 ; planning the week's menus, **YM** 27 ; poisons in nature, **FL** 68 ; preservation, **FL** 12-13 ; processing vitamin loss, **FL** 37, 39 ; requirements of the busy mother, **GF** 120 ; requirements of the elderly, **GF** 86 ; of the sick child, **GF** 113 ; sensible eating, **FL** 18 ; **UB** 61, 64, 70 ; shopping for, **FL** 31 ; storage in the home, **FL** 59 ; suspect, in foreign countries, **GT** 134 ; unsuitable for home freezing, **FL** 64 ; USDA grades, **YM** 27
Food and Drug Administration (FDA), **FL** 43
Foot sprays, **DL** 78
Force cup (plumber's helper), **FB** 55, 56
Ford, Eileen, **DL** 88
Forecast, **FT** 140
Forty-Plus Club of New York, **FT** 133
Found materials, assembly into work of art, **CF** 14
Foundation garments, **DL** 124
Foundation, make-up, and skin type, **DL** 44-45
Four-poster bed in small room, **HD** 131
Fractures, **FL** 29 ; **GF** 136
Fragrance, personal, **DL** 81
Framing of pictures, **CF** 116-119
Free arm sewing machine, **SE** 24
Freedom, of child in one-parent family, **OY** 36 ; of the single woman, **OY** 27, 88 ; to explore, in the young child, **TW** 38
Freelance work, **PY** 43
Freemasonry, **WM** 86-87
Freeze-drying of food, vitamin loss, **FL** 37
Freezer baskets, for toy storage, **HD** 114
Freezer, buying of, **YM** 64
Freezing, home, **FL** 62 ; of fruit, **FL** 60 ; of vegetables, **FL** 59 ; unsuitable foods, **FL** 64
French seam, **SE** 62, 136

Fretwork window panels, **HD** 50
Freud, on man's need for wife and lover, **SS** 18 ; on sexuality in mental and physical well-being, **SS** 38
Friendship, and marriage, **WM** 84, 88 ; female, **WM** 79 ; male, **WM** 76 ; need to earn, **KS** 139 ; of the preteener, **TW** 85 ; of the single woman, **OY** 25, 91 ; platonic, **OY** 109 ; sustaining of, **OY** 99 ; varied, **OY** 96, 98
Frigidity, **SS** 111
Frozen dinners, economic facts, **YM** 35
Frozen water pipes, management, **FB** 130
Fruit, as table centerpiece, **UT** 35 ; economy tips, **UT** 8 ; fresh, buying and using tips, **FL** 31 ; **YM** 33 ; home freezing, **FL** 60 ; in drinks, **UT** 36 ; seasons of, in economic buying, **YM** 37 (chart) ; stain, removal, **UT** 23 ; storage, **FL** 61 (table) ; supermarket sub-standard, **FL** 142
Frustration, prevention, in the toddler, **TW** 42
Fuel system, of car, **FB** 124
Fulfillment, **KS** 118 ; for the woman alone, **OY** 17, 42, 105
Fun furniture, **HD** 10-11
Fund raising, professional, **PY** 139
Funeral of parent, child's presence at, **OY** 34
Fur, buying tips, **YM** 42 ; fake, for bedspread, **SE** 77
Furnace, home, types, **FB** 79 ; repair rackets, **YM** 141
Furnishing, preparatory planning, **HD** 68 ; protective sprays, **HD** 138
Furniture, **HD** 59 ; arrangement, **HD** 70, 130 ; buying of, **HD** 137 ; **YM** 58 ; child's play room, **HD** 114 ; construction, **HD** 137 ; fix-ups, **UT** 18 ; fun, **HD** 10-11 ; grouping, **HD** 70 ; modern extensions, **HD** 14-15 ; mood-making, **HD** 66 ; refurbishing tips, **HD** 61 ; unfinished, **YM** 61, 62 ; upholstered, buying tips, **HD** 137 ; usefulness factor, in buying, **HD** 137 ; veneered, **HD** 137
Furniture polish substitute, **UT** 59
Furring strips, **FB** 44
Fuses, **FB** 59
Fusible fleece, **SE** 41, 49, 137

Fusible fleece

85

Gambling

Girls

Gambling, compulsive, **FT** 98
Game party, **UT** 29
Games, childhood, in sexual identity, **WM** 37 ;
 for children on long journeys, **GT** 138
Gang behavior, of the preteener, **TW** 85
Garage parties, **UT** 28
Garbage disposers, buying tips, **YM** 71
Gardening tips, **UT** 50
Garlic, **UB** 13
Gas leak, management, **FB** 130
Gasoline credit cards, **GT** 32 ;
 for sidewalk grass, **UT** 54
Gathering, machine, **SE** 138
Gelatin, for soft or brittle nails, **DL** 79
Gel-filled sac implant, **DL** 141
Genetic counseling, **FT** 138
Gerbils, pet, **UT** 16
German city, wall mosaic, **CF** 25
Gift wrappings, fancy, **CF** 132-133
Gingham, for placemats, **SE** 52
Gingivitis, **FL** 124
Girls, awareness of dangers of sex, **WM** 40 ;
 baby, early conditioning to

Glands

the opposite sex, **WM** 34; relationship with father, **WM** 34, 38; puberty in, **GF** 43
Glands, hormone, **UB** 26
Glass, dish, decoupage, **CF** 102; fiber, **HD** 142; shelving for windows, **HD** 54
Glass-topped table for collectors, **HD** 108
Glaucoma, routine examination for, **UB** 121
Gluing of wood joints, **UT** 19
Gold bullion, **YM** 12
Gold trinkets, **YM** 13
Golden Eagle Pass, **GT** 45
Gomez, Joan, *How not to Die Young*, **GF** 22
Gonorrhea, cure of, **SS** 141; detection by Pap smear, **SS** 143; diagnosis, **SS** 142; symptoms, **SS** 140; undetected, progress of, **SS** 140
Gored skirt, **SE** 41, 49
Gossip, sexual differences, in, **WM** 25
Government inspector, fake, **YM** 141
Grading (layering) of seam allowance, **SE** 137
Grain, fabric, definition, **SE** 136, 138, 139; straightening of, **SE** 139
Graph, for floor plan, **HD** 68
GRAS, **FL** 42
Grass stain, removal, **UT** 23
Gratitude, in the search for personal happiness, **KS** 124
Graying of hair, **FL** 122
Grease, in cesspool and septic tank, **FB** 137; in drain, clogged, remedy for, **FB** 54; mark, removal, **UT** 23
Greer, Germaine, *The Female Eunuch*, **SS** 84
Greyhound discount passes, **GT** 100
Grief, sharing of, **FT** 102
Grounding plug, installation, **FB** 70
Group behavior, of the preteener, **TW** 84; interests, and the single woman, **OY** 96; therapy, **FT** 85, 88, 143
Grout, **CF** 20
Grouting, tile, **FB** 106
Growth, of children, **FL** 26; **GF** 25
Grumman Boats, **GT** 67
Guarantee, shopping, definition, **YM** 56
Guests, care of, **HD** 93; **UT** 25, 27
Guide dogs for the blind, **FT** 140
Guidebook to Campgrounds, **GT** 46
Guidebooks, choice of, **GT** 140
Guidelines, parental, for the teenager, **FT** 49; **TW** 104
Guilt-feelings of woman, **KS** 85; **PY** 111
GUM, Moscow, **YM** 15
Gumdrop tree, **UT** 46
Gutters, periodic inspection, **FB** 133
Gymnastics, **DL** 110
Gypsumboard, **FB** 101, 104, 106, 107

Code Key			
CF:	Crafts for Fun and Profit	**OY**:	On Your Own
DL:	Discover a Lovelier You	**PY**:	A Paycheck of Your Own
FB:	The Fixit Book	**SE**:	Sew Exciting! So Simple!
FL:	Food for Life, Love, and Looks	**SS**:	The Sexual Side of Love
FT:	Family in Trouble	**TW**:	Talking With Your Child
GF:	Guarding Your Family's Health	**UB**:	Understanding Your Body
GT:	Guide to Travel and Recreation	**UT**:	Useful Tips, Hints, and Shortcuts
HD:	How to Decorate Without Going Broke	**WM**:	What Makes Men Tick
KS:	Key to Self-Understanding	**YM**:	Your Money's Worth

Hair

Hair, **DL** 54-71 ; barometer of the body, **DL** 55 ; bleaching of, **DL** 66 ; "body" makers, **DL** 58 ; brushing, **DL** 56, 58 ; care, **DL** 57 ; coloring of, **DL** 64-69 ; conditioner, **DL** 58 ; cutting of, **DL** 56, 69 ; drying, **DL** 57, 60 ; facial **DL** 35 ; fashion changes in, **DL** 10 ; graying, **DL** 56 ; growth rate, **DL** 55 ; length, determining factors, **DL** 56 ; lifespan, **DL** 55 ; mirror of health state **FL** 121 ; permanent waving, **DL** 62 ; pieces, **DL** 60-61 ; quantity, normal range, **DL** 55 ; roots, **DL** 55 ; setting, **DL** 60 ; significance, **DL** 55 ; sprays, **DL** 61 ; straightening, **DL** 63 ; streaking, **DL** 66-67, 68 ; styles, **DL** 52-63, 70-71 ; and shape of face, **DL** 68-69 ; of the teenager, symbol of independence, **TW** 105 ; styling of, **DL** 69 ; unwanted, **DL** 36, 74-77 ; washing, **DL** 56-57, 58, 138, wigs, **DL** 58-59, 62

Hairball prevention in cats, **UT** 12

Hairdresser

Hairdresser, role of, **DL** 69

"Half and half" party, **UT** 29
Hall walls, disguise of length, **HD** 135
Hallucinogens, **FT** 73 (table)
Halter-neck dress, **SE** 84
Ham, convenience-prepared, **YM** 35
Hammer, for the handywoman, **FB** 24
Hamsters, pet, **UT** 15
Hand awl, **FB** 35
Hand hem, definition, **SE** 137
Handwork, as retreat, for the busy woman, **KS** 42-43
Handyman, how to be your own, if single, **OY** 86
Hangover, mechanism, **UB** 89
Happiness, adversity as precursor to, **KS** 125; for the single woman, **OY** 126; natural, of children, **KS** 126; peaks and plateaus, **KS** 124; search for, **KS** 117
Hashish, **FT** 64, 73 (table)
Hate, in the young child, **TW** 60
Haven of the home, **FT** 27
Hazards in the home, **GF** 96-97
Head restraints in the car, **UT** 60
Health, and good looks, **FL** 115; exercise in **UB** 96; field of, jobs available, **OY** 49; of the single woman, **OY** 84
Health foods, **FL** 67; added chemicals, **FL** 69; adjunct to ordinary diets, **FL** 78
Health insurance, **YM** 107, 115; assessment of policy, **YM** 118; local, **YM** 116
Hearing, and ear cosmetic surgery, **DL** 136
Heart attack, early warning signs, **FL** 98-99; first aid, **GF** 142; beat, cessation of, first aid, **GF** 134
Heart disease, and sexual intercourse, **SS** 132; causes, **FL** 101; dieting precautions, **FL** 98; explanation of medical terms used, **FL** 100
Heart rate during sexual response, **SS** 62 (chart)
Heat loss in the home, **FB** 84
Heat marks on wood, repair, **UT** 21
Heating system, home, annual checkup, **FB** 81; economical use of, **FB** 141; fixit jobs on, **FB** 73; maintenance, **FB** 80
Height, children's averages, **GF** 27 (table)
H.E.L.P. hotline, San Francisco, **FT** 132
Hem, hand, definition, **SE** 137
Hemingway, Ernest, on impotence, **SS** 108
Henna, **DL** 13
Herbal, 12th-century, **GF** 10
Herbs, **FL** 52
Hereditary disease, genetic counseling, **FT** 138
Heroin abuse, **FT** 68, 72 (table)
Hi-fidelity system, arrangement, **HD** 70
Hiking, **GT** 109
Hiking and Hiking Trails, **GT** 110
Hippie crafts, **CF** 13
Hips, exercises for, **DL** 104-107
Historic America, weekend vacation study of, **GT** 105
Historic Inns in the U.S. **GT** 31
Hittleman, Richard, **DL** 108; **UB** 100
Hobby, of the married man, wife's exclusion from, **WM** 133; party, **UT** 29
Holes, gypsumboard, repair, **FB** 102, 106, 107; in wall, patching, **FB** 104
Hollow wall fasteners, **FB** 37
Homan, William, *Child Sense*, **GF** 29
Home(s). See also Houseboats, Trailers; as a haven, **FT** 27; buying, **YM** 82. See also House buying; checking the neighborhood, **YM** 86-87; cost comparison with home renting, **YM** 88; loans for, **YM** 102; choice of, for the single woman, **OY** 83; dangers in, **GF** 96-97; decorating. See Decorating, home; different definitions, **HD** 6-7; economy, career opportunities in, **PY** 136; extension of the personality, **HD** 16; furnishing, **HD** 59; furniture buying for, **YM** 58; improvement rackets, **YM** 140; insurance for, **YM** 119; life, in a man's ambitions, **WM** 64, 73; maintenance, minimum, **FB** 132; mobile, **YM** 92; of the single woman, **OY** 81; organization of workload, **GF** 125; personal security in, **OY** 141; precautions on leaving, **OY** 142; remodeling, financing of, **YM** 103; renting/buying cost comparison, **YM** 88 (table); safety in, **GF** 88; spreading workload in, **GF** 122
Home help, for child of the one-parent family, **OY** 65
Home theatricals, **GT** 120
Home visit by nurse, Medicare

89

Home Exchange Directory

provision for, **YM** 139
Home Exchange Directory, **GT** 59
Homecoming hours, and the teenager, **TW** 138
Homemaking, better management, **UT** 6; for the single woman, **OY** 83; freedom in, **PY** 23; in the one-parent house, **OY** 74
Homeowner's insurance. *See* Insurance, homeowner's
Home sharing, in one-parent families, **OY** 63
Homosexual man, and the single woman, **OY** 109
Homosexuality, **WM** 13; in teenagers, advice on, **FT** 134
Honesty in parent-child communication, **TW** 24; not the best policy with the divorced parent, **OY** 36; with ourselves, **KS** 18, 24
Hook, for rug-making, **CF** 42-43
Hope, Karol, on effect on children of remarriage, **OY** 122
Hormones, female sex, **UB** 18, 22; in cosmetics, **FL** 126; therapy, side effects, **UB** 142
Horse riding vacations, **GT** 71
Hose clamp, **FB** 49
Hospital work for women, **PY** 134
Hospitalization, insurance for, **YM** 115; Medicare, **YM** 138; child, **TW** 131
Hostile feelings, in the young child, **TW** 60
Hot Buttered Rum, **UT** 40
Hot water system, noisy, **FB** 139; rumbles, **FB** 84
House buying, **YM** 90. *See also* Home, buying; cost, guideline for, **YM** 97, 100; points to watch for, **YM** 94, 98-99, 101
House, exterior, weatherproofing, **FB** 87; selling of, **YM** 104; swapping, for vacations, **GT** 56; how to go about it, **GT** 59; varieties, **YM** 92-93; plants, **HD** 90
House plants, **HD** 90
Houseboat Rental Directory, **GT** 56
Houseboat, renting for vacation, **GT** 55
Houseflies, control of, **FB** 135
Household, budgeting, **YM** 18; chemicals, accidental poisoning with, **GF** 139; chores, children's help with, **OY** 74; **PY** 105; for the single working mother, **OY** 70; planning of, **OY** 72; of the working wife, **PY** 103; insect pests, control of, **FB** 134, 135 (table); linen, buying tips, **YM** 73; dye-painting, **CF** 67; labeling, **YM** 136; management, through the ages, **FB** 6-7; poisons, **UB** 82-83; skills, exploitation in seeking job for the newly single woman, **OY** 50; tidiness and the teenager, **TW** 137
Housing, for the elderly, **GF** 77
Housekeeping, better management, **UT** 6; preventive, **HD** 94
Housing, of the single woman, **OY** 81
How Not to Die Young, **GF** 22
How to Choose a Camp for Your Child, **OY** 69; **PY** 122
How to say no, for the single woman, **OY** 122
How to Use USDA Grades in Buying Food, **YM** 27
Human Sexual Response, **SS** 62
Hunt, Morton, *The World of the Formerly Married*, **OY** 121
Hurricane, precautionary measures, **FB** 132
Husband, the, **WM** 111; dual behavior, **WM** 135; enforced separation from wife, **OY** 130; how to look after, **GF** 55; loss of job, **FT** 29; neglect of, by new mother, **WM** 121; of working wife, disapproval, **KS** 135; ideal, **PY** 96; workload, **PY** 106; participation in work of the home, **WM** 135
Hygiene, feminine, **UB** 124
Hymen, in young girls, **SS** 139
Hypocrisy, in communication, **TW** 21
Hypothalamus, **UB** 23, 41
Hysterectomy, **UB** 141

Hysterectomy

Ice cream stain

Ice cream stain, removal, **UT** 23
Ice cube tray, washing, **UT** 59
Identification card, for diabetes, **FT** 139
Identification, sexual, of the preteener, **TW** 88
Identity of man with job, **FT** 31 ; of teenager, **FT** 50
Ignition, **FB** 124
Ill health, warning signals, **GF** 86
Illness, causing family stress, **FT** 103 ; child of working mother, **PY** 122 ; linked with degree of stress, **KS** 77 (chart)
Illnesses of childhood, **GF** 106 (table)
Imagination, in job research, **PY** 65 ; resulting in lying, in the young child, **TW** 79
Imitation, in babies, **TW** 34
Immunization for International Travel, **GT** 133
Immunization schedule for children, **GF** 34
Impotence, **SS** 108
Independence in adolescence, **GF** 48 ; in the toddler, **TW** 43 ; of child of working mother, **PY** 126

Indian history

Indian history, weekend

Indigestion in the elderly

vacation study of, **GT** 109
Indigestion in the elderly, diet for, **FL** 132
Individuality, in home decorating, **HD** 129; in sexual love, **SS** 124; of the child, **FT** 21; **KS** 114; **TW** 22-23, 24; of the newly single woman in society, **OY** 94; of the preteener, **TW** 84; of the teenager, **FT** 50; outside pressures on, **KS** 106
Indoor plants, **HD** 102
Industrial Designers Society of America, **PY** 138
Industrial designing, **PY** 137
Industrial solvents, addictive use, **FT** 74
Infants, feeding, on long journeys, **GT** 138; needs, in air travel, **GT** 139
Infectious diseases of childhood, **GF** 106 (table)
Inferiority feelings, **KS** 139
Infertility, **SS** 52; investigation procedures, **SS** 137
Infidelity in marriage, **WM** 140
Inflation, and investment, **YM** 120
Ingenuity, in life of the newly single woman, **OY** 27
Initiative, in relieving boredom, **KS** 70
Inkstain, removal, **UT** 23, 24
Inquiring mind, of the young child, **TW** 49
Insect bite, precaution against, **GT** 135
Insect pests, household, control of, **FB** 134, 135 (table)
Insect repellent plants, **UT** 53
Insecticides, for household pests, **FB** 134, 135 (table)
Insecurity, of the teenager, **TW** 99
Insomnia, **UB** 131
Insulation, home, **FB** 84; **UT** 60
Insulin, **FL** 107
Insurance, **YM** 107; agency, part-time, for women, **PY** 133; agents, **YM** 113; "as savings", **YM** 110; auto, **GT** 136; **YM** 132; checking before vacation, **GT** 32; claims on, **YM** 142; collision, **YM** 133; comprehensive, **YM** 133; auto, for foreign travel, **GT** 136; maximum family protection, **YM** 133; medical payments scheme, **YM** 134; saving on, **YM** 132; uninsured motorist scheme, **YM** 134; vacation, **GT** 136; brokerage, part-time, for women, **PY** 133; dental, **YM** 116; education fees, **YM** 131; fire, **YM** 119; health, **YM** 107, 115; assessment of policy, **YM** 118; local, **YM** 116; for rented property, **YM** 135; homeowner's, importance of adequate coverage, **YM** 135; package policy, **YM** 134; house and contents, **YM** 119; life, **YM** 107; conversion, **YM** 112; kinds of, **YM** 108, 109 (graph); salient points, **YM** 114; Major-Medical, **YM** 116; medical, **YM** 138; term, **YM** 108, 111 (table); through professional associations, **YM** 113; through the bank, **YM** 113
Interest, on insurance saving, **YM** 111; rates, compounding of, **YM** 23; rates of, in credit buying, **YM** 47; of various banks, **YM** 22
Interests outside the home, **UB** 50
Interior decorating, career in, **PY** 137
Intermedic, **GT** 135
Internal Revenue records, length of, **YM** 22
International Air Transport Association, **GT** 91
International party, **UT** 28
International Social Services Inc., **FT** 137
Interview, for eligibility for welfare benefit, **OY** 136; for job, **PY** 69; conduct, **PY** 71; dress sense, **PY** 71; follow-up, **PY** 77; for the single woman, **OY** 54; of "mother substitute", **OY** 65; **PY** 115
Intra-uterine device, **SS** 94
Intruder in the house, what to do, **OY** 142
Intuition, **WM** 22, 25
Investment, **OY** 139; **YM** 120
Iodine, in good nutrition, **UB** 63; in sea salt, **FL** 135
Iron, deficiency, in woman's diet, **FL** 25; dietary, **FL** 18; in good nutrition, **UB** 64
Ironing long lengths, technique, **UT** 60
Irritations, minor, in tension state, **UB** 58
Isolation, social, of the single woman, **OY** 92
Isometric exercises, **DL** 108; **UB** 100
Isotonics, **DL** 108
IUD. *See* Intra-uterine device

Jack Horner Pie, **UT** 46
Jaw, cosmetic surgery, **DL** 134
Jealousy among children, **FT** 23 ;
of parent's remarriage, **OY** 122 ;
within the family, **TW** 76 ;
husband's, **PY** 103 ; **WM** 134 ;
of mother-substitute, **OY** 60 ;
PY 117 ; of parent for teenage
child, **TW** 113
Jeep trips, **GT** 72
Jellies, contraceptive, **SS** 97
Jellyfish sting, precaution
against, **GT** 135
Jewelry, enamel, **CF** 85 ; of
polished stones, **CF** 104-107

Jobs. *See also* Career(s) ;
occupations ; clinics, **PY** 55 ;
husband's loss of, **FT** 29 ;
leads, **PY** 63 ; new, starting
out, **PY** 78 ; opportunities for
women, **PY** 25 ; part-time,
advantages to employer,
PY 37 ; for the single woman,
OY 54 ; for women, **PY** 29 ;
exchange with other
part-timers, **PY** 31 ;
opportunities in, **PY** 37 ; shared
job system, **PY** 39 ; split-level
system, **PY** 41 ; stop-gap,
FT 33 ; switching, **FT** 34 ;
temporary, **PY** 33 ; advantages,
PY 31, 35
Job hunting, **OY** 52 ; hunting
campaign, stages, **PY** 63
Jogging, **DL** 104 ; **UB** 99
Johnson, research into sexual
love, **SS** 122
Journalism, career prospects,
PY 141
Judgment, trust of one's own,
KS 54
Jumper, girl's, **SE** 37, 141
Jumping rope, **DL** 104
"Jumping the battery", **FB** 120
Juvenile court hearings, **FT** 131

Kaftan

Kaftan, **SE** 79, 142
Kasha, **FL** 136
Keeping your temper, in fixit jobs, **FB** 19
Kempe, C. Henry, on the battered child, **FT** 142
Keratin, **DL** 55
Ketchup stain, removal, **UT** 24
Kinsey, on premarital lovemaking, **SS** 78 ; research into sexual love, **SS** 122
Kitchen, decoration, **HD** 132 ; floor coverings, **HD** 39 ; lighting, **HD** 79 ; utensils, storage, **HD** 73

Kutner, Luis

Kitchenware, tips, **YM** 72
Kite making, **GT** 125
Klein, Viola, on maternal employment, **PY** 111
Kneeling cushion, in gardening, **UT** 52
Knitted garments, repair, **UT** 60
Knitting, **CF** 9 ; meeting of ends, **UT** 60
Knot, how to make, in sewing, **SE** 137 ; rya, **CF** 46-47 ; Smyrna, in rug making, **CF** 42-44
Kutner, Luis, *How to Be a Wise Widow*, **OY** 140

L-shaped room

Lampshade(s)

L-shaped room, decoration, **HD** 130
LaBarre, Harriet, *A Life of Your Own*, **OY** 112
Labeling, abuse of, **YM** 30, 34; of clothes, law on, **YM** 135; of curtain fabric, **YM** 136; of food, **FL** 36; **UT** 9
Labia, **UB** 18
Labor, sexual division of, **WM** 25; 121
Lacemaking, **CF** 12
Lace-trimmed tablecloth, **SE** 90
Lacing, tight, causing fainting, **UB** 8-9

Lactobacillus bulgaricus, **FL** 136
Lactose, **FL** 133
Ladybugs, **UT** 52
Lambert, Daniel, fattest man, **GF** 59
Lame ducks, and the single woman, **OY** 96
Laminate, plastic, repair, **UT** 21
Lamps, buying tips, **HD** 84; cord, replacement, **FB** 65; from bottles, **HD** 120; switch, repair of, **FB** 64, 65
Lampshade(s), batik, **CF** 79; crochet, **HD** 125; enamel-covered, **CF** 80-84;

Landscape architecture

macrame, **CF** 115; making, **HD** 85; with pressed dried grasses, **CF** 95
Landscape architecture, **PY** 137
Language, development, in children, **TW** 34; nonverbal, **TW** 21; of love, **SS** 43-44; of sex education in very young children, **TW** 52
Lanolin, in cosmetics, **FL** 126
Lantern jaw, cosmetic surgery for, **DL** 134
Latch hook, for rug making, **CF** 42-43
"Latch-key" children, **OY** 62
Launderette, nighttime dangers of, to the single woman, **OY** 142
Laughter, therapeutic value of, **GF** 84
Lawn, care of, **UT** 54
Laxatives, abuse of, **UB** 85
Layering (grading) of seam allowance, **SE** 137
Layette for baby, **SE** 61-69
Layoff, general company, **FT** 39
Leaky faucets, repair of, **FB** 49; pipes, repair of, **FB** 47, 48; roof, emergency repair, **FB** 130
Learning, in the child, **TW** 10-11, 73
Leather thonging, for bead necklaces, **CF** 20, 31; for polished stone jewelry, **CF** 106
Leavening agents, **FL** 107
Leaving the house, precautions to take, **OY** 142
Leftovers, disposal of, for the overweight, **FL** 120; storage, **UT** 6
Legitimacy, and the contraceptive pill, **SS** 24
Lemon, in cosmetics, **FL** 126; in drinks, **UT** 36
Lengthwise-of-grain, definition, **SE** 138
Leonardo da Vinci, anatomical drawing of woman's body, **UB** 7
Lethargy, in adolescence, **GF** 47
Letter of application, for job, **PY** 66-69
Levator muscles, **SS** 134
LH. *See* Luteinizing hormone
Librarian, children's, work of, **PY** 130
Library of Congress, Division for the Blind and Physically Handicapped, **FT** 140
Life expectancy, **UB** 136
Life Insurance, **YM** 107; conversion, **YM** 112; kinds of, **YM** 108, 109 (graph); salient points, **YM** 114
Life of Your Own, A, **OY** 112
Lifeline, social agency, **FT** 135
Lifespan through the ages, **GF** 74 (chart); **UB** 136; woman's, **PY** 24
Lifestyle, in buying a home, **YM** 85
Lifetime reserve, definition, **YM** 139
Lifting, correct, **UB** 110
Light and color, interaction, **HD** 77
Lighting, buying tips, **HD** 79; camping equipment, **GT** 41; dining room, **HD** 132; economy tips, **UT** 56; in the home, **HD** 77; outdoor, **HD** 84; overhead, **HD** 132; practical factors, **HD** 77; switches, **HD** 82, 84
Linen, household. *See* household linen
Line, in fashion, **DL** 126
Lines, facial, meaning of, **KS** 84
Lingerie, **DL** 123; **YM** 42
Lining a coat, **SE** 66
Linoleum, **HD** 47
Lipid, **FL** 100, 101
Lipoproteins, **FL** 102, 126
Lipstick, **DL** 50, 51
Liquor, economic buying of, **YM** 36
Listener, the, in marriage, **WM** 130
Listening, art of, **TW** 17; to the teenager, **TW** 111; to yourself, **KS** 46
"Live and let live" in self-understanding, **KS** 54
Liver, cooking, **FL** 48; **YM** 28; effect on, of excessive alcohol, **UB** 89; spots on hands, **DL** 80
Living alone, incidence, **OY** 19
Living-dining room, separation of areas, **HD** 130
Living room, lighting, **HD** 80
Load funds, **YM** 126
Loan associations, **YM** 22
Loan, National Defense, for college purposes, **YM** 131
Lobster, as centerpiece, **UT** 35
Lochia, **SS** 134
Lock wrench, **FB** 25, 27
Locks, on the home of the single woman, **OY** 141
Logic, of fixit jobs, **FB** 18
Loneliness, of the single woman, **OY** 91; of unemployment, **FT** 32; sexual, of the single woman, **OY** 105
Loner, of the preteens, **TW** 87

Longevity

Longevity, inherited, **UB** 137

Loop

Loop, thread, definition, **SE** 139
Loss of job, **FT** 29; **WM** 73
Love and marriage, changing modern patterns of, **SS** 76; and permissive sex, **SS** 40; and the single woman, **OY** 102; as distinct from desire, **SS** 33; blindness of, **WM** 98; communication of, to the child, **TW** 26; extra-marital, **SS** 70, 80; family, **GF** 18; in adolescence, **WM** 92; in lovemaking, **SS** 69; language of, **SS** 42-43; man's declaration of, **WM** 90, 94; meaning of, to woman, **WM** 92, 94; mother-child, **TW** 8-9; of lifelong friends, **OY** 99; psychology of food in, **FL** 126; romantic, joy of, **WM** 100; second time around. *See* Remarriage; sexual, the magic ingredient, **SS** 33; teenage, **TW** 111; varieties of, for the single woman, **OY** 104; Victorian attitudes, **SS** 12-13
Love affair, commitment in, **SS** 84; extra-marital, **SS** 70, 80; of the newly single woman, **OY** 112
Lovemaking, erotic embellishments of, **WM** 139; experimental, before marriage, **SS** 74; in marriage, incidence of, **SS** 86; wife's attitude to, **WM** 138, 139; without loving, for the single woman, **OY** 105; woman as initiator, **SS** 66, 69
Loveplay, **SS** 66
Lovers, **SS** 6-7
Low-residue diet, **FL** 130
LSD (Lysergic acid diethylamide), **FT** 68; abuse, **FT** 73 (table)
Lubricants for sticking windows, **FB** 93
Lullaby, original definition, **GF** 11
Lumps in the breast, **UB** 140
Lung-heart resuscitation, **GF** 134
Luteinizing hormone (LH), **UB** 24
Lutheran Social Service, **FT** 136

Lying

Lying, in the young child, **TW** 78

Code Key				
CF:	Crafts for Fun and Profit		**OY:**	On Your Own
DL:	Discover a Lovelier You		**PY:**	A Paycheck of Your Own
FB:	The Fixit Book		**SE:**	Sew Exciting! So Simple!
FL:	Food for Life, Love, and Looks		**SS:**	The Sexual Side of Love
FT:	Family in Trouble		**TW:**	Talking With Your Child
GF:	Guarding Your Family's Health		**UB:**	Understanding Your Body
GT:	Guide to Travel and Recreation		**UT:**	Useful Tips, Hints, and Shortcuts
HD:	How to Decorate Without Going Broke		**WM:**	What Makes Men Tick
KS:	Key to Self-Understanding		**YM:**	Your Money's Worth

Machine basting

Man

Machine basting, definition, **SE** 138
Machine gathering, definition, **SE** 138
Macrame, **CF** 17, 108-115; marketing of, **CF** 138
Macrobiotic diet, Zen, **FL** 77
Magazine Publishers Association, **PY** 141
Mail, while abroad, **GT** 140
Mailbox, name on, for the single woman, **OY** 141
Mailed merchandize, unordered, **YM** 143
Major-Medical Insurance, **YM** 116
Make-up, first experiments with, **DL** 18; following facelift, **DL** 138; history, **DL** 41; psychology of, **DL** 52; 20th-century, **DL** 44; variation with mood and time, **DL** 52-53
Making-up stages, **DL** 40
Malnutrition, in obesity, **UB** 62; of wrong eating habits, **FL** 116
Man, *See also* Father, Husband; and marriage, **WM** 104-108; companionship with man, **WM** 12; competitiveness,

Managing your Health

WM 62; divorced, incidence, OY 22 (chart); emasculation by woman, KS 57; fattest recorded, GF 59; "helpless", WM 131; ideal cast of females, WM 56-57; ideal weights for, GF 60 (table); identity through occupation, WM 59, 66; in love, WM 90, 96; influence over, of woman, WM 8; living alone, incidence, OY 19; magazines for, WM 108; making of, WM 44; married, WM 111; incidence, OY 22 (chart); meeting, for the single woman, OY 107; modern, pressures on, GF 55; mystique of, WM 46; occupation of, WM 59-75; psychological difference from woman, WM 19; role of, in intersexual relationships, WM 46; romanticism of, WM 111, 114, 119; single, incidence, OY 22 (chart); storage, HD 113; "strong and silent", WM 131; widowed, incidence, OY 22 (chart)
Managing Your Health, UB 97
Manhattans, mixing, UT 39
Manicure, home, DL 78-79
Man made fibers, HD 139-143 (table)
Man's robe, SE 57
Map making, neighborhood, GT 125
Margarine, FL 39; YM 32
Margolius, Sidney, *Consumer's Guide to Better Buying,* YM 35
Marijuana, FT 64; abuse, FT 73 (table); UB 11; harmful or harmless? TW 142; law on, TW 143
Marital status, statistical analysis, OY 22 (chart)
Market research, part-time career for women, PY 133
Marketing of crafts, CF 138; business or craft? CF 141
Marriage, FT 115; WM 102-109. *See also* Mating; remarriage; and friendship, WM 84, 88; as an adventure, SS 50; as normal framework of life, OY 19; as proof of man's maturity, WM 108; as working partnership, PY 10-11; changing state of, KS 93, 97; communication in, SS 57; companionship in, SS 57; conflict in, WM 131; counseling, FT 126; PY 131; agencies, FT 137; critical phases, FT 115; WM 116; disillusionment in, WM 116; division of responsibilities in, WM 112-113; double standard of, WM 117; early, SS 76; expectations v reality, FT 116; first, as learning experience, OY 120; flexibility in, FT 118; incidence with age, OY 117; infidelity in, FT 8-9, 124; SS 83; WM 140; man's view of, WM 115; modern concept of, SS 15; money problems, FT 120; WM 137; mutual freedom within, SS 51; mutual needs in, WM 126; non-consummation of, SS 113; of opposite temperaments, KS 37, 119; of the pregnant teenager, FT 54; parent's, effect on child's future marriage, KS 133; permanence of, SS 45; possessive element of, WM 118; problems, need for outside help, FT 126; relationships, for working couple, PY 109; rewards of, FT 126; second, *see* remarriage; self-analysis in, WM 123; sex in, WM 126; sex, in, difficulties, FT 123; inertia, SS 117; monotony, SS 117; successful, ingredients for, WM 125; teenage, FT 116; through the ages, OY 14-15; triple identity, WM 129; unequal growth of partners, FT 124; woman's view of, WM 115; working wives, PY 96; young, "emotional transfer" of child from parent, FT 119
Married life, desire for, OY 118
Married man and the single woman, OY 115; incidence, OY 22 (chart)
Married woman, as full-time student, PY 56; incidence, OY 22 (chart); varied role of, WM 111; working, PY 96
Martin, Clement, UB 97
Martini, mixing, UT 38
Masking tape, for odd needlework threads, UT 60
Masonry drilling, FB 40, 41
Masonry fasteners, FB 38, 40
Masters, research into sexual love, SS 122
Masters and Johnson, *Human Sexual Response,* SS 62

Masters and Johnson

99

Masturbation

Masturbation, as preparation for sexual love, **SS** 60, 117, 130; in adolescence, **TW** 139; in children, **SS** 138; **TW** 134
Materialism, **KS** 108
Materials. *See also* Fabrics; for wall decoration, **HD** 26
Mating, beginnings of, **SS** 33; choice available for, **WM** 52; woman's attitude in, **SS** 33
Mattress, choice of, **HD** 60
Mature years, wisdom of, **KS** 126
Maturity, in sexual love, **SS** 122; physical, in adolescence, **TW** 139
Mayonnaise, substitute for furniture polish, **UT** 59
Meals, number and timing, for proper nutrition, **FL** 139; planning, **FL** 142; **OY** 73; regular, for the diabetic, **FL** 112; revolving, **UT** 28
Measurements, body, in dressmaking, **SE** 140; before buying furniture, **HD** 68; for carpeting, **HD** 42; of walls, for home decorating, **HD** 32
Measuring, spoons, **UT** 7; tools, **FB** 29
Meat, cooking, **FL** 56; cuts, cooking time, **FL** 47; economical buying, **FL** 140; **UT** 9; **YM** 27; home freezing, **FL** 64; home storage, **FL** 63 (table); variety, **FL** 48; **UT** 11; **YM** 28
Medicaid program, **YM** 138
Medical checkups, **GF** 55; **UB** 114
Medical costs of children, parent's responsibility for, **OY** 135
Medical services, **YM** 138
Medical technology, career in, **PY** 134
Medical treatment, authorization, **GF** 142
Medical-surgical insurance, **YM** 115
Medicare program, **YM** 138; voluntary medical plan, **YM** 139
Medicine(s), accidental poisoning of children, **GF** 91; administration, in the sick child, **GF** 114
Medicine chest, contents, **GF** 102-103
Medieval romantic love, **SS** 36
Menopause, **UB** 32; definition, **UB** 133; duration, **UB** 134; sex life in, **UB** 135; symptoms, **UB** 133; timing of, **UB** 134
Menstrual cycle, **SS** 95; **UB** 25 (diagram); effect on emotions, **UB** 16; in adolescents, **GF** 43; irregularities, **UB** 30; physical discomfort in, **UB** 19 (bead chart)
Menstrual flow, capacity, **UB** 30
Menstrual symptoms, age factor in, **UB** 32
Menstruation, **UB** 18; conception during, **SS** 132; duration, **UB** 30; influencing factors, **UB** 30; instruction on, to the preteener, **TW** 92; intercourse during, **SS** 132; onset, **GF** 43; **UB** 139; painful, relationship with premenstrual tension, **UB** 32; resumption after pregnancy, **SS** 134; society's attitudes to, **UB** 29; superstitions surrounding, **UB** 31
Mental alertness, relationship with physical exercise, **KS** 73
Mental health, advice and information, **FT** 142; counseling, **PY** 132
Mental Health Centers, Community, **FT** 142
Mental hospital, commitment laws, **FT** 143
Mental illness, **FT** 109; **UB** 47
Mental retardation, advice and information, **FT** 141
Mental stimulation, for the toddler's mother, **KS** 134
Mercury, sublimate, ingredient of olden-day cosmetics, **DL** 42
Mensendieck System, **DL** 108, 110
Mescaline, **FT** 68
Mesh backing, for rug making, **CF** 42-43
Metallic fiber, **HD** 143
Metchnikoff, Ilya, **FL** 136
Methadone abuse, **FT** 72 (table)
Michelin Green/Red Guides, **GT** 140
Middle age, sexual pleasure in, **SS** 82, 84-85
Middle-age man, fresh employment, **FT** 133
Migraine, relaxation exercises for, **UB** 55
Mildew mark, removal, **UT** 24
Mileage, daily, recommended maximum for car travel, **GT** 27
Milk, economy tips, **UT** 7; **YM** 29, 30; non-fat dry, **YM** 29; stain, removal, **UT** 23

Milk

Millet, **FL** 136
Mind and body, interrelationship, **FT** 97
Mineral oil preparations, affecting vitamin absorption, **UB** 87
Minerals, food intake, **FL** 18; in good nutrition, **UB** 63
Mirror frame, mosaic, **CF** 25
Mirror tiles, **HD** 130
Miscarriage, depression following, **SS** 136; repeated, risk of, **SS** 135; risks of, **SS** 133; subsequent conception, **SS** 135
Mistakes in life, learning from, **KS** 111
Mitered corner, **SE** 80, 82, 92, 94
Moaning, persistent, **KS** 140
Mobile homes, buying of, **YM** 92; multi-level, **YM** 94
Mobiles, **CF** 120-125; Christmas, **CF** 127, 136
Modacrylic, **HD** 143
Moisturizer, **DL** 30, 32, 45
Mold stand, for candle making, **CF** 48
Molding, husband's, of wife, **KS** 22; on doors, **HD** 99; wall, **HD** 36
Moles, **DL** 35
Molly bolts, **FB** 38, 39
Momma, **OY** 122
Money. *See also* Banks; Finance; Insurance; Investment; Loan; declining purchasing power of, **YM** 19; evolution, **YM** 8-9; management, **YM** 16; personal allowance, for the teenager, **TW** 106; private borrowing, **YM** 50; problems, in enforced separation of husband and wife, **OY** 133; in marriage, **FT** 120; **WM** 137; mirror of emotional problem, **FT** 123; spending, for vacations, **GT** 130
Money lending, **YM** 50
Monosodium glutamate, **FL** 107
Monotony, in housewifery, **KS** 65; in married love, **SS** 58, 117
Montezuma's Revenge, **GT** 134
Mood(s) of room, **HD** 66; of teenagers, **TW** 100; of woman, **SS** 106; restless, **KS** 130
Morality, advice to teenagers, **TW** 140
Mortgage, **YM** 100; outstanding, 1970, **YM** 103; types, **YM** 102 (table)

Mosaic work, **CF** 18-25;
Mosquitoes, control of, **FB** 135
Motels, **GT** 30
Moth, clothes, control of, **FB** 135
Mother, care of herself, **GF** 120; interests outside the home, **GF** 122, 125; mood of, effect on family, **GF** 126; multifarious jobs, **PY** 47; new, neglect of husband, **WM** 121; of the small child, need for mental stimulation, **KS** 134; role in the family's health, **GF** 14-15, 17; self-fulfillment within the family, **GF** 20; single working, **OY** 59; unmarried, advice and information for, **FT** 135; working, **GF** 20; **PY** 111; **WM** 142; advantages of, **KS** 73; and her child, **PY** 14-15; husband's disapproval, **KS** 135; incidence, **PY** 18; of school age children, **KS** 135; reentrance into business, **PY** 33; single, **OY** 59
Mother substitute, **OY** 60, 62; **PY** 113
Mother-baby relationship, **TW** 30
Mother-child relationship, **OY** 60; **TW** 8-9
Motherhood, new, **TW** 29
Mother-in-law, hold of, over son, **WM** 132
Mothers Anonymous, for parents of battered children, **FT** 142
Motor, of heating system, **FB** 80
Motorhomes, **GT** 39
Mouth deodorants, **UB** 121
Mouth-to-mouth resuscitation, **GF** 133
Mouthwashes, **DL** 78
Moving, of books, **UT** 56
Mudstain, removal of, **UT** 24
Muesli, **FL** 69
Mulching, **UT** 52
Mural(s), decoupage, **CF** 102; through the ages, **HD** 8-9
Mushrooms, freshly. canned, **FL** 141
Musical festivals, as vacation destinations, **GT** 81; in the home, **HD** 92
Musical instruments, homemade, **GT** 122
Muscle tone, improvement with exercise, **DL** 100
Mustard stain, removal, **UT** 24
Mutual funds, **YM** 124, 126
Mystic, Connecticut, **GT** 106
Mystique, of the sexes, **WM** 28

101

Nail(s)

National Defense loan

Nail(s), care of, **DL** 78-80; common, **FB** 33; finishing, **FB** 33; sizes, **FB** 34; types, **FB** 33, 34
Nail polish, **DL** 80
Nail pop, **FB** 102
Nail set, **FB** 35
Nailing procedure, **FB** 24, 25, 34, 35
Name, change, of child, through adoption by parent's remarriage partner, **OY** 123; of new wife, **KS** 22
Nap (pile) of fabric, definition, **SE** 138

Napkin, for finger food, **UT** 31
Narcotics, **FT** 72 (table)
National Association for Retarded Children, **FT** 141
National Association of Mental Health, **FT** 142
National Association of Real Estate Boards, **PY** 140
National Center for Prevention of Child Abuse and Neglect, **FT** 142
National Council on Alcoholism, **FT** 132
National Defense loan, for college purposes, **YM** 131

National Education Association

National Education Association, **PY** 130
National Forest Service, camping facilities, **GT** 46
National Foundation-March of Dimes, **FT** 138
National Heart and Lung Institute, **FL** 102
National Merit Scholarships, **YM** 131
National Nutritional Foods Association, **FL** 70
National Organization for Women, **PY** 94
National parks, camping facilities, **GT** 44; noncamping accommodation, **GT** 31; skiing in, **GT** 77
National Rehabilitation Counseling Association, **PY** 132
National Vocational Guidance Association, **PY** 131
National Welfare Rights Association, **OY** 137
National Wilderness Preservation System, **GT** 46
National Wildlife Refuge System, The, **GT** 113
National Trail System, **GT** 110
Nature trail, underwater, **GT** 66
Necklaces, bead, **CF** 27-35; marketing of, **CF** 138
Needles for home sewing, **SE** 25
Nefertiti, Queen of Egypt, **DL** 6, 41
Negro Almanac, The, Ploski & Kaiser, **FT** 133
Neighborhood map making, **GT** 125
Neighborliness, for the single woman, **OY** 142
Nervous system, **UB** 36, 40
Neutering of cats, **UT** 13
New England, cradle of American history, **GT** 106
New York Stock Exchange, **YM** 122-123
New York University Hospital, **DL** 132
Newspapers, in job research, **PY** 64
Night driving, **FB** 126
Nightgown, baby's, **SE** 69
Nightlife on vacation, cost of, **GT** 131
Nightmares, children's, **GF** 36; **TW** 62
Nipples, inverted, **UB** 140
"No", how to say, for the single woman, **OY** 112
Noise, of home appliances, deadening, **UT** 56
No-load funds, **YM** 126
Nonpayment of support money, **OY** 135
North American Bike Atlas, **GT** 112
Nose, cosmetic surgery for, **DL** 132; in character of the face, **DL** 133
Notch, definition, **SE** 138
Nourishing creams, **DL** 32
Nudity in parents, effect on children, **SS** 139
Nursery schools, **OY** 66; **PY** 118
Nursing, following breast cosmetic surgery, **DL** 141; home, of the elderly, **GF** 76; training for, **PY** 134
Nursing home custodial care, insurance for, **YM** 138; for the elderly, **GF** 77
Nutrients, basic, in beauty aids, **FL** 126
Nutrition, effect on the whole woman, **UB** 62; minimum daily requirements, **UB** 66-67 (table)
Nylon, **HD** 142-143

Nylon

Code Key			
CF:	Crafts for Fun and Profit	**OY:**	On Your Own
DL:	Discover a Lovelier You	**PY:**	A Paycheck of Your Own
FB:	The Fixit Book	**SE:**	Sew Exciting! So Simple!
FL:	Food for Life, Love, and Looks	**SS:**	The Sexual Side of Love
FT:	Family in Trouble	**TW:**	Talking With Your Child
GF:	Guarding Your Family's Health	**UB:**	Understanding Your Body
GT:	Guide to Travel and Recreation	**UT:**	Useful Tips, Hints, and Shortcuts
HD:	How to Decorate Without Going Broke	**WM:**	What Makes Men Tick
KS:	Key to Self-Understanding	**YM:**	Your Money's Worth

Oatmeal face masks

Occupations

Oatmeal face masks, **FL** 126
Obesity, **DL** 83; **FL** 81; and heart disease, **FL** 104; as cause of disease, **GF** 58 (chart); definition, **UB** 72; in adolescence, **GF** 46; in children, **GF** 30; in diabetes, **FL** 110; in men, **GF** 56; in menopause, **UB** 135; in pregnancy, dangers, **FL** 29; incidence, **UB** 72; malnutrition in, **UB** 62
O'Brien, Patricia, on being a woman alone, **OY** 78
Obscene language in children, **UT** 47; telephone calls, **OY** 142
Observance, in family life, **KS** 143
Occupations. *See also* Career(s); Jobs; father's, in childhood aspirations, **WM** 38; husband's, wife's ambition in, **WM** 141; in man's role in life, **WM** 59-75; in working off anger, **UB** 56; loss of, **WM** 73; of man, integration with family life, **WM** 67-68; of mother of school age children, **KS** 135; for the single woman, **OY** 42; market

Occupational Outlook Handbook

available, **OY** 48-49, 50; part-time, **OY** 54; qualities needed, **OY** 45; woman's, as social enterprise, **PY** 22; changes in, **FB** 14-15; through the ages, **PY** 6-7; pressures of, 70; stress in, effect on health, **GF** 66; wife as husband's "business asset" in, **WM** 143
Occupational Outlook Handbook, **PY** 52, 70
Occupational therapy, training in, **PY** 135
Odor in plastic container, removal, **UT** 58
Office of Federal Contract Compliance, Employment Standards Administration, **PY** 90
Off-stage jobs in theater, **PY** 143
Oil, bath, water-soluble, **DL** 75; glands, of the hair follicle, **DL** 55
Oilcloth place mats, **UT** 30
Oily complexion, care of, **DL** 28
Ointment, contraceptive, **SS** 97
Old age. *See* Elderly, the
Old Fashioned, mixing, **UT** 39
Old people, famous, **GF** 84-85. *See also* Elderly, the
Old Person in Your Home, The, **GF** 75
Old Sturbridge Village, **GT** 106
Older woman, day care of children, **PY** 114
Older Women, In Praise of, **DL** 24
Oldest recorded person, **UB** 137
Olefin polypropylene, **HD** 141
Olive oil, dilution, **UT** 9
Once-in-a-lifetime vacations, **GT** 91
One-parent family, the, **OY** 29
Openness, in marital disagreements, **KS** 142
Operation, cosmetic. *See* Cosmetic surgery
Opiates, **FT** 72 (table)
Oral sex play, risk of, during pregnancy, **SS** 133
Orange juice, source of vitamin C, **FL** 134
Order-chaos struggle in family life, **KS** 112, 140
Organ meats, **FL** 48; **UT** 11; **YM** 28
Organic food production, **FL** 72
Organizations for the single, **OY** 108; secret, **WM** 86-88
Orgasm, absence, in sex life, **SS** 131; causing ovulation, **SS** 95; delay, in man, **SS** 69; failed, **SS** 60; frequency, in woman, **SS** 130; in masturbation, **SS** 130; intensity, **SS** 130; multiple, **SS** 63, 130; of woman, **SS** 69; role of the brain in, **UB** 38; timing of, in man, **SS** 69
Orgasm, The Function of the, **SS** 39
"Other woman", in history, **SS** 10-11
Other people's problems, cure for personal worries, **KS** 83
Our Bodies, Our Selves, **DL** 16
Outdoor clubs, **GT** 77
Outdoor lighting, **HD** 84
Outlet, wall, replacement, **FB** 68-70
Ovaries, egg content, **UB** 143; function, **UB** 18
Overcasting, definition, **SE** 138
Overdose of drugs, treatment, **GF** 140
Overnight guests, **HD** 93; hiking, **GT** 109
Overprotectiveness, of the newly single parent, **OY** 35
Oversensitivity, **KS** 141
Overweight. *See* Obesity
Ovolacto vegetarian diet, **FL** 75
Ovulation, **SS** 95; **UB** 24
Oxalic acid crystals, **FB** 108

Code Key			
CF:	Crafts for Fun and Profit	**OY:**	On Your Own
DL:	Discover a Lovelier You	**PY:**	A Paycheck of Your Own
FB:	The Fixit Book	**SE:**	Sew Exciting! So Simple!
FL:	Food for Life, Love, and Looks	**SS:**	The Sexual Side of Love
FT:	Family in Trouble	**TW:**	Talking With Your Child
GF:	Guarding Your Family's Health	**UB:**	Understanding Your Body
GT:	Guide to Travel and Recreation	**UT:**	Useful Tips, Hints, and Shortcuts
HD:	How to Decorate Without Going Broke	**WM:**	What Makes Men Tick
KS:	Key to Self-Understanding	**YM:**	Your Money's Worth

Pacific Crest Trail

Pacific Crest Trail, **GT** 110
Package tours, **GT** 92 ; "hidden costs", **GT** 130 ; varieties, **GT** 94 ; what to look out for, **GT** 98
Packages, mailing technique, **UT** 58
Packaging of food, **FL** 33
Packing, for family vacation, **GT** 139
Padding, carpet, **HD** 44
Pain, menstrual, **UB** 32 ; of eyelift, **DL** 138 ; of ovulation, **UB** 24
Paint(s), application, **HD** 33 ; in home decorating, **HD** 28 · mark, removal, **UT** 24 ; stirring, **FB** 30 ; **HD** 32
Painted bottles, **CF** 36-39
Painting(s) as investment, **YM** 12 ; for children, **GT** 123 ; therapeutic, **CF** 17
Paintwork, periodic inspection, **FB** 133
Pap smear, **UB** 119, 143
Paper creche, **CF** 128-131
Paperweight, in clear plastic, **CF** 56-60

Paraffin wax

Paraffin wax, for candle making, **CF** 48

Paraphernalia

Paraphernalia in the home, apportioning space for, **HD** 18
Parasympathetic nervous system, **UB** 40
Parent(s), ambition for teenager, **TW** 116; aping of teenager in dress and manner, **TW** 122; attachment of child of opposite sex, **TW** 56; guiding authority, **TW** 62; authority, teenager's challenge of, **TW** 100; communication with child, **FT** 18; example of, in child rearing, **TW** 24; on sexuality, **TW** 94; fallibility, acknowledgment to the child, **TW** 22; getting away together, **GF** 70; in child's marriage, **FT** 120; interest in teenage activities, **TW** 113; late teenager's view of, **TW** 125; of teenagers, preparation for being alone again, **TW** 126; part in child's school life, **TW** 73; temporary separation from child, **TW** 130; time spent with children, **FT** 20; values, as guide to teenagers, **FT** 49
Parents Without Partners, **OY** 40
Parent-child conflict, in young childhood, **TW** 44; relationship, in adolescence, **GF** 52
Parenthood, last throes, **TW** 126; single-handed, **OY** 29
Parent-teacher relationship, **TW** 70
Parent-teenager relationship, **TW** 138; breakdown, **TW** 125; trouble spots in, **TW** 105
Parkinson's Law, on employment, **PY** 37
Parsons table, **HD** 104
Partnership, in marriage, **PY** 10-11
Partner-swapping, **SS** 84
Parts, fitting together, in fixit jobs, **FB** 18
Part-time work. See Job, part-time
Party, children's, **UT** 44; invitations, **UT** 25; punches, **UT** 40
Party giving, techniques, **UT** 25
Passe-partout, **CF** 117
Passport, how to obtain, **GT** 102; lost, procedure, **GT** 141
Patchwork, **HD** 123
Paternity, and the contraceptive pill, **SS** 24
Paths of woman's life, **KS** 26-26 (diagram)

Patterned fabric through the ages, **SE** 12-13
Patterns, dressmaking, variations in, **SE** 141; in room decoration, **HD** 34
Pawn shop, **YM** 50-51
Paycheck, of the part-timer, **PY** 30
Peanut butter, **FL** 70; **UT** 9
Peck, Gregory, on the necessity for challenge in the teenager, **FT** 48
Penicillin, treatment of venereal disease, **SS** 141
Penis, size and sexual satisfaction, **SS** 131
People, "working with", jobs available, **OY** 48
Peptic ulcer, diet for, **FL** 131
Perennials, **UT** 53
Perfume, **DL** 80-81
Perishable foods, home storage, **FL** 62
Permanent waving, **DL** 62
Permissiveness, sexual, dangers of, **SS** 40
Personal allowance, for the teenager, **TW** 106; habits, in marriage, **FT** 117; inventory, **PY** 45, 50; reappraisal, of the newly single woman, **OY** 23; relationships at work, **PY** 80, 83; safety, for the woman alone, **OY** 141; security, of the single woman, **OY** 86
Personality, development through crises, **OY** 23; growth in, through trial, **FT** 113; **OY** 120; in home decorating, **HD** 88; in homemaking, for the single woman, **OY** 84; in job seeking, **PY** 52; reflected in the home, **HD** 16
Perspiration mark, removal, **UT** 24
Pesticides, effect on food, **FL** 44
Pests, insect, household, control of, **FB** 134, 135 (table)
Pets, **GF** 98-99; **UT** 10
Petting, heavy, as preparation for marriage, **SS** 77; in marriage, **SS** 66
Phillips screwdriver, **FB** 24
Phobias, **FT** 109; group therapy, **FT** 143
Photography, career prospects in, **PY** 142
Physical contact with very young child, preparation for later love, **TW** 55

Physical therapy

Physical therapy, training in,

107

Physician's assistant PY 135
Physician's assistant, work of, PY 134
Pickle liquid, in marinating, UT 8
Picture framing, CF 116-119; HD 110; hanging, technique, FB 38; making, HD 110; windows, dressing, HD 49
Piggy bank, YM 11
Pile (nap) of fabric, definition, SE 138
Pill, the. *See* Contraceptive pill
Pills, diet, DL 84; FL 138
Pillow cover, patchwork, HD 123
Pilot, hole, in fixit jobs, FB 34, 35, 36, 37; in floorboards, FB 116, 117; light of gas furnace, FB 81
Pimples, DL 35
Pincus, Gregory, discoverer of the pill, SS 89
Pin money work at home, PY 43
Pipe clamp, FB 48, 49
Pipe wrench, FB 26
Pipes, leaky, repair of, FB 47, 48
Pituitary, UB 23
Place cards, in pressed flowers, CF 95
Placemats, SE 52; UT 59
Planned parenthood, FT 57, 134
Planned Parenthood Federation of America, Inc., FT 135;
Planning, family vacations, GT 17; house routine, of the working wife, PY 105; of life, KS 96
Plantation punch, UT 40
Planters' Punch, UT 39, 40
Planting, choice of site, UT 53
Plants, as garden screens, UT 52; cuttings, UT 54; decoration of windows, HD 50; indoor, HD 90, 102; as table counterpiece, UT 35; care of, UT 54; flowering, UT 54; rotation, UT 53; watering, UT 54
Plastering, repairs, FB 101
Plastic, clear, setting in, CF 56-63; for mounting clippings, UT 59; laminates, repair, UT 21; surgeons, DL 130
Plate of ceramic tile sheeting, CF 25
Plateau, in reducing diet, FL 138
Platonic friendship, for the single woman, OY 109
Play groups, OY 66; PY 118
Play of children, as outlet for expression, FT 20; development, TW 62
Play room, arrangement, HD 114
Play schools, OY 66
Playtime trousers, SE 96; adaptation for different sizes, SE 143; with fly front, SE 142
Pleasure cruising, GT 98
Pliers for the handywoman, FB 26
Plug, appliance, FB 63; grounding, installation, FB 70; replacement, FB 60, 61, 63; rewiring, FB 61, 62
Plumber's helper (force cup), FB 55, 56
Plumbing, for the handywoman, FB 47; noisy system, FB 139; periodic inspection, FB 133
Plywood, for shelving, FB 42
Pocket money, for children's help in the house, OY 74; for the teenager, TW 106; for vacations, GT 130
Poe, William, GF 75
Poisoning, accidental, GF 138; HD 94; in children, GF 91; in the elderly, GF 98; diagnosis, GF 139
Poisons, UB 81; definition, GF 138; in natural foods, FL 68
Police department sales, UT 56
Polished stones, CF 104-107
Polyester, HD 141; jersey, for wraparound skirt, SE 28
Polygamy, WM 116
Polystyrene beads, for cushion chair, SE 113
Pop festivals, sexual freedom at, SS 38-39
Port, outlet clogged, remedy for, FB 54
Portuguese Man-O'-War, GT 135
Post Office sales, UT 56
Posture, UB 105
Potatoes, convenience-prepared, comparative costs, YM 35; plants, UT 51
Pots and pans, buying tips, YM 72; cleaning tips, UT 59
Pottery, CF 10, 13; ancient Peruvian, CF 15
Poultry, economical buying, UT 9
Powder, cosmetic, DL 49
Power system, of car, FB 124
Practicing what you preach, in teaching young children, TW 81
Praise, importance of, in rearing young children, TW 42
Praying mantis, in garden, UT 52

Preferences

Preferences, in personal inventory, **PY** 52
Pregnancy, after cessation of periods, **UB** 135; air travel in, **GT** 133; exercise during, **SS** 137; explanation to first child, **TW** 132; ideal age for, **SS** 137; in the married teenager, courses of action, **FT** 55; in the unmarried teenager, **FT** 54; motivation for, **SS** 101; nutritional requirements, **FL** 28; postnatal, **SS** 135; sexual desire of woman in, **SS** 133; sexual intercourse during, **SS** 133; syphilis in, **SS** 143; tests, **SS** 136; unwanted, advice and information, **FT** 135
Premarital lovemaking, **SS** 77; as introduction to promiscuity, **SS** 79
Premenstrual tension, effect on behavior, **UB** 26 (chart), 28; relationship with painful periods, **UB** 32
Preservation of food, **FL** 12-13, 39
Preshrinking of fabric, **SE** 26
Pressing, accessories, in home sewing, **SE** 24
Pressure, academic, on the teenager, **TW** 117
Preteeners, **TW** 83; effect of outside influence on the home, **TW** 94
Prevention of illness, **UB** 112
Preventive housekeeping, **HD** 94
Privacy of the newly single parent, **OY** 36; of the teenager, **TW** 104
Professional associations, insurance facilities, **YM** 113
Professional Photographers of America Inc., **PY** 143
Professionalism, **PY** 80
Progesterone, **UB** 24
Projects, home, **HD** 95
Promiscuity, **SS** 34; advice to teenagers, **TW** 140; early experiences causing, **SS** 79
Promotion tactics, **PY** 82-88; techniques, for marketing of craft work, **CF** 140
Protein, **FL** 18; in good nutrition, **UB** 62; in vegetarian diets, **FL** 77; requirements, in growth periods of children, **FL** 26; top dozen buys, **UT** 9
Prowler in the home, what to do, **OY** 142
Pruden, Bonnie, **DL** 102
Psilocin, **FT** 68
Psilocybin, **FT** 68
Psychedelic drugs, **GF** 50 (table)
Psychiatric help, need for, incidence, **FT** 107
Psychiatrist, differentiation from psychologist, **FT** 143
Psychologist, differentiation from psychiatrist, **FT** 143
Psychology, in the beauty business, **FL** 126
Psychosis, following LSD abuse, **FT** 68
Psychosomatic illness, **UB** 36, 46
Puberty, **GF** 41; age of onset, **TW** 93; approaching, instruction on, **TW** 92; sexual awareness in, **WM** 51
Public relations, career opportunities, **PY** 138
Public Relations Society of America, **PY** 139
Publishing and applied arts, jobs in, **OY** 48; **PY** 142
Punch, recipes, **UT** 40
Punishment, of the young child, **TW** 40
Puppet show, home, **GT** 121
Puppy fat, **GF** 46
Puritanism, **SS** 34
Pyke, Magnus, on poisonous natural foods, **FL** 68

Pyke, Magnus

Code Key			
CF:	Crafts for Fun and Profit	**OY:**	On Your Own
DL:	Discover a Lovelier You	**PY:**	A Paycheck of Your Own
FB:	The Fixit Book	**SE:**	Sew Exciting! So Simple!
FL:	Food for Life, Love, and Looks	**SS:**	The Sexual Side of Love
FT:	Family in Trouble	**TW:**	Talking With Your Child
GF:	Guarding Your Family's Health	**UB:**	Understanding Your Body
GT:	Guide to Travel and Recreation	**UT:**	Useful Tips, Hints, and Shortcuts
HD:	How to Decorate Without Going Broke	**WM:**	What Makes Men Tick
KS:	Key to Self-Understanding	**YM:**	Your Money's Worth

Quarrels

Quilting bee

Quarrels and quarreling, need for, to clear the air, **KS** 142 ; in marriage, **GF** 22-23 ; **WM** 131 ; with neighbors, **KS** 137
Questions of children, how to answer, **TW** 49
Quilting bee, **CF** 16

Rabbits

Reducing

Rabbits, as pets, **UT** 16
Rack, for stemware, **UT** 58
Rackets, **YM** 140
Radiators, bleeding, **FB** 81
Rail tours, **GT** 96
Rail travel, European, **GT** 100
Rain, driving in, **FB** 126
Rainy day activities, **GT** 118
Rainy weather starting, of the car, **FB** 120
Raising agents, **FL** 107
Ranch vacations, **GT** 69
Rat race, materialistic, **KS** 108
Rayon, **HD** 139
Reaction of child to loss of parent, **OY** 34
Real estate, career in, **PY** 140
Rebellion in the toddler, **TW** 42
Recipe party for bride-to-be, **UT** 28
Recreational vehicle (rec vee, RV), **GT** 38
Reducing, **DL** 83. *See also* Obesity; clubs, **DL** 87; diets, **FL** 85 et seq., 137; **UB** 77; for children, **GF** 32; for husbands, **GF** 56; plateau stage, **FL** 138; exercise in, **UB** 96; five points for, **DL** 88; sexual intercourse in, **SS** 132

Reference Guide for Travelers

Reference Guide for Travelers, **GT** 140
Referral racket, **YM** 140
Refrigerators, **FL** 35; **YM** 64
Registry of Medical Technologists, American Society of Clinical Pathologists, **PY** 135
Rehabilitation counseling, **PY** 132
Reich, Wilhelm, on sexuality in mental and physical well-being, **SS** 39
Relaxation, art of, **GF** 120; **UB** 55
Religion, and sex, **SS** 27
Remarriage, **KS** 100; **OY** 113; and wife's support money, **OY** 135; effect on children, **OY** 122; incidence, **OY** 117; of the divorced, **FT** 126; reasons for, **OY** 118; success rate, **OY** 119
Remodeling of house, **YM** 103
Rented homes, **YM** 88; insurance for, **YM** 135; vacation, **GT** 48, 54
Reorganization of life to avoid irritations, **UB** 58
Repair of body tissue, **FL** 17
Repairs rackets, **YM** 141
Reprisals, discrimination, **PY** 94
Research, in job campaign, **PY** 63
Respect, mutual between teenager and parent, **TW** 102
Respiration, artificial. *See* Resuscitation
Responsibility, of the single woman, **OY** 76
Restlessness, personal, **KS** 120, 130
Resume, role in job hunting, **OY** 53, 55; **PY** 57-61
Resuscitation, **GF** 133; lung-heart, **GF** 134
Retarded child, the, help for parents, **FT** 141
Reticence, social, of the newly single woman, **OY** 92
Retirement, Social Security benefit in, **OY** 139; **YM** 136
Revival of the unconscious, **GF** 140
Revolving meal, **UT** 28
Rewards, for teenage achievements, **TW** 108
Rhogam, **FT** 138
Rhythm, importance to the young child, **TW** 34
Rhythm method of contraception, **SS** 95
Rice, **FL** 136
Ripping, **FB** 26
Rise-and-fall lamps, **HD** 80
Risks, role in prevention of boredom, **KS** 73
Rivalry, child, within the family, **TW** 76
Road safety, instruction in, to young children, **GF** 94
Robe, bath, doll's, **SE** 130; man's, **SE** 57
Rocks for the rock garden, **UT** 53
Roller, paint, **HD** 33
Roman Catholic Church and contraception, **SS** 94
Romance, **SS** 36-37; **WM** 100-101
Roof leaks, emergency repair, **FB** 130; periodic inspection, **FB** 133; repair racket, **YM** 141
Room(s) divider, **HD** 119, 131; dual use, **HD** 23; large, division, **HD** 131; mood, **HD** 66; private, of the teenager, **TW** 137; style, **HD** 64; three-in-one, **HD** 119
Rose, gift-wrapping, **CF** 126, 133
Rosenthal, M. S., **GF** 50
Rouge, **DL** 46, 47
Roughage, shortage, in modern diets, **FL** 72
Routine of home care, escape from, **UB** 52
Royal Canadian Air Force exercises, **UB** 98
Rubber gloves, protective, **DL** 79
Rug making, **CF** 40-47; **HD** 46
Rug weaving, **CF** 10-11; Persian, **CF** 14
Rugs, **HD** 46; anti-slip devices, **HD** 137; buying of, **YM** 63
Rule, folding wooden, **FB** 30
Running stitch, definition, **SE** 138
Russell, Bertrand, on romantic love, **SS** 36, 38
Rust mark, removal, **FB** 108; **HD** 133; **UT** 24
Rusting steel windows, **FB** 94
RV (recreational vehicle, rec vee), **GT** 38
Rya knot, **CF** 46-47; rugs, **CF** 45-47

Rya knot

Saccharin

Saving(s)

Saccharin, **FL** 110, 133
"Safe" period, **SS** 95
Safety in the home, **GF** 88; **HD** 93; personal, for the woman alone, **OY** 141; rules, for camping, **GT** 46
Sailing vacations, **GT** 62
Salary, discussion of, in job application, **PY** 76; of the working wife, **PY** 100
Salem Witch Museum, **GT** 106
Sale(s), auction, **YM** 60-61; bargain calendar, **YM** 80-81; clothes, **YM** 38, 40; police department, **UT** 56; Post Office, **UT** 56; types of, **YM** 40; warehouse, **YM** 58
Salt-restricted diet, **FL** 105
Sand-casting, of candles, **CF** 54
Sanding, attachment of drill, **FB** 30-31; of wooden floors, **FB** 110
Sanforized fabric, **SE** 26
Sangria punch, **UT** 40
Saran, **HD** 143
Saving(s), banks, **YM** 22; favorite American institutions, **YM** 25; how they grow, **YM** 24 (graph); in insurance, **YM** 110; rewards of, **YM** 18;

113

Sawing

tips on, **YM** 24 ; with term insurance, **YM** 111
Sawing, technique, **FB** 27
Saws for the handywoman, **FB** 26, 27
Scalds, first aid, **GF** 137
Scarf, batik, **CF** 79 ; tie-dyed, **CF** 68-73
Scarring, following body lifts, **DL** 143 ; following breast reduction, **DL** 143 ; from burns, **GF** 138 ; from eyelifts, **DL** 138 ; in breast cosmetic surgery, **DL** 141
Scatter cushions, **SE** 118
Scholarships, **YM** 131
School, achievement, of the teenager, **TW** 108 ; child's entry into, **TW** 64 ; mother's adjustment, **TW** 70 ; competition in, **TW** 74 ; counselor, work of, **PY** 131 ; parent's part in life of, **TW** 73 ; preparation for, by parent, **TW** 67 ; return to, of the newly single woman, **OY** 50 ; vacations, and children of working mothers, **OY** 69
Scissors, for home sewing, **SE** 24
Scratched wood, renovation, **UT** 19
Screening, garden, of plants, **UT** 52 ; medical, **FL** 102 ; **GF** 56 ; window, home repairs, **FB** 142, 143
Screwdrivers for the handywoman, **FB** 24
Screwing, technique, **FB** 35
Screws, expansion-type, **FB** 38, 39 ; sizes, **FB** 36 ; wood, **FB** 34
Scuba diving, **GT** 66
Sculpture, **CF** 9
Sea salt, **FL** 135
Seam allowance, definition, **SE** 139 ; layering (grading), **SE** 137
Seam, finish of, **SE** 136
Sebaceous glands, **FL** 121
Secondhand, cars, buying of, **YM** 74, 76-77 ; law on, **YM** 75 ; clothes, buying of, **YM** 40 ; furniture, buying of, **YM** 60
Securing of stitching lines, **SE** 139
Securities, kinds of, **YM** 123
Security, personal, of the single woman, **OY** 86
Security Investors Protective Corporation, **YM** 126
Self-appraisal, in beauty, **DL** 20, 22
Self-appreciation, lack of, **KS** 40-45
Self-assessment, **KS** 34 ; **OY** 23
Self-awareness, of the nine-year-old, **TW** 83
Self-care, of the single woman, **OY** 84
Self-confidence, building up, **KS** 40 ; in woman, **KS** 20 ; **PY** 46
Self-criticism, hyper- **KS** 45 ; leading to oversensitivity, **KS** 141
Self-delusion, **KS** 37
Self-doubt, of the teenager, **TW** 99
Self-enhancement, **DL** 24
Self-esteem, in children, **TW** 25 ; of the teenager, and his sexual behavior, **TW** 112
Self-exploration, for the single woman, **OY** 126
Self-image, **DL** 16 ; **UB** 75, 78
Self-knowledge, **FT** 104 ; **PY** 44 ; **UB** 48
Self-preservation, emotional necessity of, **KS** 18
Self-recognition, **KS** 34
Self-reproach, **KS** 86
Self-respect, **KS** 53
Self-understanding, **KS** 17
Selling, jobs available in, **OY** 49
Selvedge, definition, **SE** 139
Seminal emissions, **TW** 93
Sensitivity, excessive, **KS** 141 ; of baby to mother's mood, **TW** 29
Sensory deprivation, research on, **KS** 65
Sensuality, cultivation of, in woman, **SS** 117
Sensuous Woman, The, **SS** 60
Separation, agreement, financial problems, **OY** 134 ; enforced, of husband and wife, **OY** 130 ; from loved ones, stress caused by, **KS** 83
Septic tank, maintenance, **FB** 137 ; periodic inspection, **FB** 133
Service entry, for electricity, **FB** 59
Services, the, friendship within, **WM** 82
Serving cart, with pressed flower decoration, **CF** 91, 94
Sewage, home, **FB** 137
Sewing accessories, **SE** 24 ; machines, **SE** 23 ; **YM** 70 ; key to, **SE** 140 ; terms, glossary, **SE** 136

Sex. *See also* Lovemaking ; act of, Victorian attitude to, **SS** 34 ; woman's equal partnership in,

Sexes SS 20; and religion, SS 27; and the menopause, UB 135; and the teenager, TW 139; and your child, SS 138; as a sin, SS 26; dangers of, awareness in girls, WM 40; determination before birth, SS 135; discrimination, in credit rating, OY 138; education, of the very young children, TW 51; of the preteener, TW 89; of the teenager, TW 141; extra-marital, SS 70; free, at pop festivals, SS 38-39; hormones, female, UB 18, 22; in conflict with western upbringing, SS 28; in marriage, WM 126; instinct of, SS 28; man's objective view of, WM 93; modern public attitude to, SS 40; myths of, SS 129; offenders, warning against, to young children, TW 135; organs, describing to the very young child, TW 52; pre-marital experience of WM 40

Sexes, the fundamental differences, WM 16, 22; inequality of WM 20; physical differences, child's acceptance of, WM 37; reversal of roles, WM 22, 28-29; traditional role of, WM 19

Sexual appetite in marriage, SS 45; arousal, SS 64-65, 66; awareness, dawning of, WM 51; behavior, double standard of, SS 23; of the teenager, TW 111; desire, in pregnancy, SS 133; periodic variation in, in woman, SS 132; difficulties in marriage, FT 123; experience, first, SS 73, 76-77; in American college girls, incidence, SS 73; in teenagers, advice on, TW 141; exploration, in young children, TW 135; feeling in children, SS 138; freedom, SS 17; fulfillment, determining influences, SS 84; for the single woman, OY 105; pressures for, SS 30

Sexual, identification, of the preteener, TW 88; family teaching of, WM 36-40; impulse, lifespan of, SS 81; inequality, WM 20; inertia in marriage, SS 117; intercourse, "afterglow", in women, SS 63; calorie expenditure in, SS 132; during menstruation, SS 132; during pregnancy, SS 133; explanation to the very young child, TW 53, 54; frequent, reducing chance of conception, SS 137; in heart trouble, SS 132; painful, SS 131; resumption of, after childbirth, SS 133; organs, female, UB 18; performance, effect of age, SS 120; pleasure as an acquired art in women, SS 58; in middle age, SS 82; 84-85; potency, vitamin E in, FL 134; prowess, and vitamin A, FL 134; reactions of women, variation in, SS 62; responsiveness, role of the brain, UB 38

Sexual Behavior in the Human Female, SS 63

Sexual love, antidote to stress, GF 70; art of, SS 126; as a communication, SS 109, 126; depressing factors in, SS 106; individuality in, SS 124; lifespan of, SS 118; maturity in, SS 122; modern woman's preparation for, SS 104; postnatal aversion to, SS 110; spiritual aspects, SS 126; without orgasm, SS 131; woman's view of, SS 70; malfunction, SS 108; monotony in marriage, SS 48

Sexuality, in mental and physical well being, SS 38-40

Shades, roll-up, HD 52

Shadow puppets, GT 122

Shakespearean companies, GT 85

Shampoos, DL 56-57, 58; dry, DL 61

Shared jobs, in part-time work, PY 39

Shaving of leg hair, DL 74, 76

Sheets, as curtains, HD 57; as tablecloths, UT 30; as wall covering, HD 36; buying tips, YM 73

Shelving, HD 72; disguise for bad wall surface, HD 135; fixing, FB 40; technique, FB 42, 43, 44, 45; glass, for windows, HD 54; materials for, FB 42; standards, alignment, FB 45; wall, HD 21

Shimming of door hinge, FB 90

Ship model in clear plastic, CF 61

Shirring, SE 47, 63

Shirts, buying tips, YM 43

Shock, electric, treatment, GF 141; treatment, GF 132

Shoe polish stain, removal, UT 24

Shoelaces, anchorage of knot,

115

Shoes

Shoes, buying tips, **DL** 124; **UT** 58; **YM** 42; for babies, **UT** 61; harmful to the feet, **UB** 9; toes, loosening, **UT** 56
Shopping abroad, bargaining, **GT** 131; around the world, **YM** 14-15; comparison, **FL** 141; co-operative, **YM** 36; for food, **FL** 31; for dieters, **DL** 88; lists, for the single working mother, **OY** 72; planning, of the working wife, **PY** 105
Short circuit, **FB** 59
Shortcomings of one's family, acceptance of, in relief of stress, **UB** 59
Shorts, doll's, **SE** 131
Shower curtains, **HD** 133
Shrinkage, allowance for, in curtain buying, **HD** 57
Shutters, **HD** 137; periodic inspection, **FB** 133; window, **HD** 52
Shyness, **KS** 138
Sickle cell anemia, genetic counseling, **FT** 138
Siebert, Muriel, first woman stockbroker, **YM** 121
Sierra Club, **GT** 46, 77
Sightseeing. *See also* Tourism; research for, **GT** 28
Silicone, in cosmetic surgery, **DL** 133, 134, 141
Silverfish, control of, **FB** 135
Single man, incidence, **OY** 22 (chart); living alone, incidence, **OY** 19
Single woman, the, **OY** 18. *See also* Widowed woman, the; and the married man, **OY** 115; as working mother, **OY** 59; "builder" or "coper"? **OY** 78; emotional reaction to new single state, **OY** 22; financial problems, **OY** 134; in the "couple-oriented" world, **OY** 24; incidence, **OY** 22 (chart); incidence of marriage, by age, **OY** 119 (chart); living alone, incidence, **OY** 19; individuality, **OY** 24; meeting men, **OY** 107; organizations for, **OY** 108; remarriage, **OY** 113; sense of purpose, **OY** 20, 42, 78, 126; social status, **OY** 24; taxes, **OY** 138; through the ages, **OY** 6-7, 12-13
Sink, clogged, remedy for, **FB** 54, 55
Ski Touring Council, **GT** 77
UT 61

Ski Touring Guide, **GT** 77
Skiing, cross-country (ski touring), **GT** 75; vacations, **GT** 72
Skill, hidden, **KS** 131
Skin, bath care of, **DL** 75; blemishes, **DL** 34; changes with age, **DL** 28; chemopeel, **DL** 139; dermabrasion, **DL** 138; healthy, balanced diet for, **FL** 140; mirror of health state, **FL** 120; texture, **FL** 120; type, and facelifts, **DL** 136; bath essence for, **DL** 75; determination of, **DL** 28
Skinny physique, problems, **FL** 92
Skirt, doll's, **SE** 129; evening, of brocade, **SE** 71; flared, **SE** 41; fluted, **SE** 49; wraparound, **SE** 28, 141
Slapping, **TW** 40-41
Sleep, amount necessary, **GF** 32; **UB** 130; in adolescence, **GF** 48; in health and beauty, **UB** 15; purpose of, **UB** 130; requirements of adults, **GF** 70; role of the brain in, **UB** 40-41
Sleeping bags, **GT** 40
Sleeplessness, **UB** 131
Sleepwalking, in children, **GF** 36
Slipcovering furniture, **HD** 60, 61, 63, 64
Sloe Gin Fizz, **UT** 39
Small business, **FT** 133; **PY** 56
Small Business Administration, **FT** 133
Small talk, **KS** 137
Smear test, **UB** 119
Smell, sense of, after nose surgery, **DL** 133
Smoking, age risks of, **GF** 67 (table); giving up, **GF** 61; ill effects of, **UB** 92; in adolescence, **GF** 52; of electrical appliance, **FB** 73
Smyrna knot, **CF** 42-44
Snake, plumber's, **FB** 55, 56
"Sniffing" of industrial solvents, **FT** 74
Snoring, **UB** 132
Snorkeling, **GT** 65
Snow party, **UT** 46
Soap and water washing, for oily skins, **DL** 28, 30
Soap, for dry complexions, **DL** 30; spray, for garden pests, **UT** 53
Social Contract, The, Robert Ardrey, **FT** 97
Social intercourse, art of, **KS** 138
Social isolation, of the single woman, **OY** 92

Social isolation

116

Social life

Social life of parent, in one-parent family, **OY** 36
Social occupations, jobs available, **OY** 48
Social security, **YM** 136
Social security, benefits, age coverage, **YM** 137; on retirement, **OY** 139; **YM** 136; earnings-benefits rule, **YM** 137; outline of, **YM** 137
Social welfare resources, in handicap, **FT** 104
Social work, for the single woman, **OY** 124
Society, and the woman temporarily separated from her husband, **OY** 132
Socket wrench, **FB** 50
Socks, buying tips, **YM** 43
Sodium, high-content foods, **FL** 109; in good nutrition, **UB** 63
Soft drink stain, removal, **UT** 24
Soft toys, dye-painted, **CF** 67
Solitary child, the, **TW** 87
Solitude, fear of, **KS** 133
Solvent soluble paint, **HD** 28
Sorbitol, **FL** 110, 133
Sound, absorbency factor, in floor coverings, **HD** 40; in the home, **HD** 91
Soundproofing in the home, **HD** 136
Soup, economical buying, **UT** 6
Souvenir hunting, pitfalls, **GT** 132
Spa, **UB** 13
Space management in the home, **HD** 74, 130
Spackle, **FB** 101
Spandex, **HD** 141-142
Spade bit, for hand drill, **FB** 28
Spanish embroidery, **CF** 12
Spanking, **TW** 40-41
Spare-time profit schemes, **PY** 43
Spathe flower, **UT** 54
Spaying of cats, **UT** 13
Speaking Out, **FT** 140
Spectacles, eye make-up for, **DL** 49
Speech, baby's first attempts at, **TW** 33; of deaf children, advice and information, **FT** 140; therapy, training in, **PY** 135
Speed, addiction, **FT** 71
Sperm, ancient view of, **UB** 7
Spices, **FL** 53; **UT** 9
Spider mites, **UT** 53
Spiders, control of, **FB** 135
Spinning wool, **CF** 12
Spinster, the, **OY** 18. *See also* Single woman, the
Split-level jobs, in part-time work, **PY** 41
Spooning method, of candle making, **CF** 53, 55
Sports, calorie values, **GF** 63 (table); vacations, **GT** 61
Sportsmanship, in children, **UT** 48
Spot reduction, by exercise, **UB** 105
Sprays, insecticide, for household use, **FB** 134, 135 (table)
Squeaking floors, **FB** 114; stairs, **FB** 138
Stabilizers, food additives, **FL** 41
Stain removal, **UT** 22-25; on wood, **UT** 21
Stained glass windows, do-it-yourself, **HD** 54
Stainless steel tableware, buying tips, **YM** 72
Stairs, squeaky, **FB** 138
Standards, shelf, **FB** 40; alignment, **FB** 45; fastening techniques, **FB** 42
Staple foods of the world, **FL** 6-7
Star, foil, **CF** 127, 134
Starting procedure, car, **FB** 119
Stay Young Longer, **DL** 100; **UB** 94
Stay-stitch, definition, **SE** 139
Stealing, in the young child, **TW** 76
Steaming, as deep cleanser for the face, **DL** 30
Stearic acid, for candle making, **CF** 48
Steering system, of car, **FB** 125
Stemware, storage, **UT** 58
Sterilization, contraceptive, **SS** 98
Sticking doors, **FB** 89; drawers, **UT** 18
Stimulants, **FT** 73 (table); **GF** 50 (table)
Stitches, definition, backstitch, **SE** 136; blanket, **SE** 136; running, **SE** 138; stay-stitch, **SE** 139
Stitches, sewing machine, **SE** 22-23
Stitching, lines, securing of, **SE** 139
Stock, cooking, **FL** 54
Stock, definition, **YM** 123; investment in, **YM** 120
Stock broker, definition, **YM** 125
Stock Exchange, New York, **YM** 122-123

Stock Market

Stock Market, how to follow,

117

Stomach

Stomach **YM** 124, 125
Stomach, reduction, cosmetic, **DL** 143
Stoneground products, **FL** 72
Stones, polished, **CF** 104-107
Storage, man, **HD** 113; space in the home, **HD** 72
Storm damage to windows, **FB** 95; windows, **UT** 56
Storytelling, **GT** 122
Stowe Cross-country Ski Club, **GT** 76
Straight-of-grain, definition, **SE** 139
Straight stitch sewing machine, **SE** 23
Straightening of end of fabric, **SE** 139
Stranger, anxiety, **TW** 130; warnings against, to young children, **TW** 135
Stratford, Ontario, Shakespeare productions, **GT** 85
Straw matting, **HD** 47
Stress, **FT** 95; **UB** 45; and illness, units system, **FT** 101; danger signals, **FT** 104; effect on fingernails, **FL** 123; effect on health, **GF** 66; emotional, producing digestive disorders, **UB** 43; family, preventive measures, **FT** 102; sources, **FT** 100; how to deal with it, **UB** 48; illnesses, incidence, **FT** 97; in children, **FT** 110; **GF** 110; in growth of personality, **FT** 113; **OY** 120; incontinence, **UB** 139; indicated by excessive masturbation, in the young child, **TW** 134; of puberty, **TW** 93; points, linked to life events, **KS** 77 (chart)
Stretch marks in pregnancy, reduction of, **SS** 137
String art, **CF** 86-88
Stringing of beads, **CF** 28-29
Striped fabric, for sundress, **SE** 107
Striptease, in arousing husband's excitement, **SS** 64-65
Stroke, first aid, **GF** 142
Student, demonstrations, legal rights, **FT** 130; loan programs, **YM** 131
Studio apartment, division, **HD** 131
Studs, wallboard, locating, **FB** 42, 43
Study area in the home, **HD** 92
Style, furniture, combinations, **HD** 66, 134
Style, hair. *See* Hair, Style; of room, **HD** 64
Suburban living, for the single woman, **OY** 82
Success, as proof of manhood, **WM** 63, 73
Sugar, addiction, **FL** 139; danger to body chemistry, **FL** 139; harmful effects on teeth, **GF** 38; restriction, **FL** 112; **GF** 60; substitutes, **FL** 133
Suggestion, in management of the toddler, **TW** 45
Suicide, in adolescence, **FT** 112; potential, warning signs, **FT** 113; prevention centers, **FT** 143
Summer camp, for the one-parent child, **OY** 69
Sun, excessive, effect on hair, **DL** 61
Sun dress, doll's, **SE** 133; swingaround, **SE** 107
Sunburn, **GT** 134
Sun tanning, effect on the skin, **DL** 32
Super Economy Guide to Europe, **GT** 140
Supermarket shopping, **FL** 141; economic, **YM** 30
Support, parental, for the teenager, **TW** 104
Support, money, effect of remarriage, **OY** 135; in assessment for welfare benefit, **OY** 137; nonpayment, **OY** 135; of divorcee and her children, **OY** 134
Survival kit, for the handywoman, **FB** 21, 22
Suspension system, of car, **FB** 125
Swaddling of babies, **UB** 8
Swap, the, **YM** 7
Sweeteners, **FL** 133; artificial, **FL** 110; addiction to, **FL** 139
Swimming, for exercise, **DL** 107; health value of, **UB** 97; instruction, **GT** 62
Swindlers, how to avoid, **YM** 140
Swing needle sewing machine, **SE** 23; automatic, **SE** 24
Switch, lamp repair of, **FB** 64, 65; on long cord, **FB** 66; wall, replacement, **FB** 66, 67, 68
Sympathetic nervous system, **UB** 40
Syphilis, cure of, **SS** 141; detection in blood, **SS** 142; latest stage, **SS** 141; second stage, **SS** 140; symptoms, **SS** 140; transmission to unborn baby, **SS** 143

Syphilis

Table

Table, adaptable, **HD** 104; collector's, **HD** 108, decorations, **UT** 30
Tablecloth(s) homemade, **SE** 90; **UT** 30
Tableware, stainless steel, buying tips, **YM** 72
Tacking, definition, **SE** 139
Tact, definition, to the young child, **TW** 80
Tai-Chi, **DL** 108, 110
Tailor tacking, definition, **SE** 139
Talcum powder, accidental inhalation, **UT** 61

Tax

Talent, latent, **KS** 131

Talking, learning by babies, **TW** 33; of parakeets, **UT** 15; to plants, **HD** 90
Tampons, sanitary, **SS** 139
Tank, hot water, rumbling, **FB** 84; septic, maintenance, **FB** 137; periodic inspection, **FB** 133
Tanners and tanning, **DL** 32
Tape, lifting, of wallboard, **FB** 102; measure, flexible steel, **FB** 29
Tapestry, French, **CF** 10
Taste, in the elderly, **FL** 29, 132
Tax, for the single and married,

Tea

Tea OY 138; in house-exchange, YM 105; on money earned from crafts, CF 142; records, and retaining of canceled checks, YM 22
Tea, harmful effects, UB 81
Tea ball, for spices, UT 9
Tea stain, removal, UT 22
Teacher, in preschool center, OY 68
Teacher-child relationship, TW 70
Teacher-parent relationship, TW 70
Teaching, of crafts, CF 140; partnership arrangement, PY 130; quality of, in day care centers, PY 119; returning to, PY 130
Teen Clinics, FT 134
Teenagers. *See also* Adolescence; activities, parental interest in, TW 113; advice to, on contraception, TW 139; on morality, TW 140; alcoholism, FT 131; and sex, TW 139; care of, GF 41; communication with, TW 99; confidants outside the family, TW 113; drug abuse in, FT 63; TW 112, 142; homecoming hours, TW 138; homosexuality in, advice, FT 134; keeping his room tidy, TW 137; later, view of parents, TW 125; love in, TW 111; marriage of, FT 116; problems, through the ages, FT 10-11; reckless driving by, FT 131; relationship with parents, TW 138; sexual behavior, TW 111; share in family chores, TW 137; social pressure on, FT 76; stress in, FT 112; unsocial behavior, FT 43; vacations for, GT 89; addresses, GT 142
Teeth, children's, GF 36, 38; effect on, of diet, FL 123; routine care of, UB 121
Telephone, family, use of by teenagers, TW 107
Telephone book, name in, for the single woman, OY 141
Television, antenna, periodic inspection, FB 133; for the sick child, GF 118; noise factor, HD 91; repair rackets, YM 141
Temper, in fixit jobs, FB 19
Temperament, KS 37; TW 30
Temperature, at ovulation, UB 24; child's, GF 107; in home floor coverings, HD 40; normal ranges, GF 108
Temporary work, OY 54; PY 33; advantages, PY 31, 35
Tension, signs of, at puberty, TW 93
Tents, camping, GT 36
Term insurance, YM 108, 111 (table)
Termites, FB 136; YM 99
"Terrible twos", TW 42
Terry cloth, for beach tote, SE 33; for man's robe, SE 57; curtains HD 57
Tests, for venereal disease, SS 141; pregnancy, SS 136
Texture, clothes, and figure type, DL 124
Thalamus, UB 41
Thawing, of frozen water pipes, FB 130
Theater, off-stage job prospects, PY 143; vacations, GT 84
Theatricals, home, GT 120
Theft, car, GT 35. *See also* Burglary
"Theme" parks, GT 115
Thermometers, GF 107
Thermostat, of home furnace, FB 79, 80
Thighs, cosmetic reduction of, DL 143; exercises for, DL 108-111
"Think thin", DL 89
Thinness, excessive, diet for, DL 91
Thread count, on linen labels, YM 136
Thread loop, definition, SE 139
Three-in-one room, HD 119
Thrift Rail Pass, GT 101
Thrift shops, YM 40, 61
Thrombosis, FL 100
Thrombus, FL 100
Tidiness and the teenager, TW 137
Tie-dyeing, CF 68-73
Tile joints, FB 107
Tile sheeting, CF 25
Tiles. *See also* Mosaic work; acoustical, HD 136; carpet, HD 136; ceramic, as wall covering, HD 36; flooring, FB 108; HD 47; mirror, HD 130; repair; FB 105; wall, HD 36, 133
Time, for family communication, FT 20; proper use of, for the single woman, OY 86; spent with children, FT 20
Tipping, on a cruise, GT 98
Tips. *See under specific subjects*
Tire changing procedure, FB 122
Tired wife, the, KS 61; UB 47

Tired wife

Tiredness

Tiredness, on long car trips, **GT** 35
Tissue repair of the body, **FL** 17
Titillation, **SS** 64, 66
Tjanting, **CF** 74
Tobacco smoking, risks of, **TW** 143
Tocopherol, **FL** 41, 135
Toddlers, accidents in the home, **GF** 91
Toddy, **UT** 39
Toilet, clogged bowl, remedy, **FB** 56; repair, **FB** 52; flushing, insufficient, remedy, **FB** 53; system, mechanics, **FB** 50; whistling, repair of, **FB** 52
Toilet training, influence on later sex life, **SS** 139
Tom Collins, mixing, **UT** 39
Tomatoes, growing tips, **UT** 51
Tools, for drilling holes, **FB** 28; for fixit jobs, **FB** 20; for the handywoman, buying tips, **FB** 24; nonessential, **FB** 21, 24; for home plumbing, **FB** 47
Tornadoes, procedure in, **FB** 132
Tourism. *See* Sightseeing
Tourist Board addresses, **GT** 144
Tourniquet, **GF** 130
Towel rack, fixing technique, **FB** 37
Towels, buying tips, **YM** 73
Toys, storage, **HD** 74
Trailer and Camping Guide, **GT** 46
Trailer park, **YM** 95
Trailers, **YM** 92; camping, **GT** 38
Training, occupational, for the newly single woman, **OY** 50
Tranquilizers, abuse, **FT** 72 (table)
Transformations in home decorating, **HD** 132
Transformer, doorbell, **FB** 71
Translating, career prospects in, **PY** 142
Trapp Family Lodge, Vermont, **GT** 76
Travel, air, economic, **GT** 91; by car, **GT** 24; for the single woman, **OY** 126; with young children, **GT** 137
Travel agency career, **PY** 139
Travel agents, **GT** 92
Travel sickness in young children, **GT** 137
Traveler's checks, **YM** 22-23
Traveling through the ages, **GT** 12-13
Tray, decoupage, **CF** 94-101
Triacetate, **HD** 140
Trichomonas infection, **UB** 139
Triglycerides, **FL** 100, 101, 102
Triple Irish Chain pillow cover, **HD** 123
Trousers, doll's, **SE** 131; playtime, **SE** 96; adaptation for different sizes, **SE** 143; with fly front, **SE** 142
Truth, shades of, for the young child, **TW** 80
Truth in Lending Act, **YM** 50
T-shirt, tie-dyed, **CF** 73; to own design, **CF** 64-66
Tumble polishing, of stones, **CF** 104
Tumor, fibroid, **UB** 141; of the breast, **UB** 120
Tunic, from kaftan pattern, **SE** 142
Turkey, economic buying of, **YM** 29
"Turkey wattle", **DL** 134
Turtles, as pets, **UT** 16
TV. *See* Television
Tweezers, eyebrow, **DL** 35
Twiggy, **DL** 22
Twin foetuses, **TW** 52-53
"Twins a year apart", **SS** 95

Two-way switches

Two-way switches, **HD** 84

Code Key				
CF:	Crafts for Fun and Profit		**OY**:	On Your Own
DL:	Discover a Lovelier You		**PY**:	A Paycheck of Your Own
FB:	The Fixit Book		**SE**:	Sew Exciting! So Simple!
FL:	Food for Life, Love, and Looks		**SS**:	The Sexual Side of Love
FT:	Family in Trouble		**TW**:	Talking With Your Child
GF:	Guarding Your Family's Health		**UB**:	Understanding Your Body
GT:	Guide to Travel and Recreation		**UT**:	Useful Tips, Hints, and Shortcuts
HD:	How to Decorate Without Going Broke		**WM**:	What Makes Men Tick
KS:	Key to Self-Understanding		**YM**:	Your Money's Worth

Understanding

Uterus

Understanding, in communication, **TW** 18
Underweight, problem in adults, **FL** 92
Underwriters' Laboratories Inc., (UL, ULI), **YM** 68
Unemployment, **FT** 29; area, **FT** 39; emotional reaction, **FT** 31; sudden, turned to good advantage, **FT** 36; wife's moral support, **FT** 40
Universal jaws, of hand drill, **FB** 28
Unmarried woman, **OY** 18. *See also* Single woman, the

Unused capabilities of woman, **KS** 30
Upholstered furniture, buying tips, **HD** 137
Upholstery fabric, buying tips, **UT** 59
Urban planning, training in, **PY** 138
Uretha, **UB** 18
Urine, production, and "water pills", **UB** 91
USDA (U.S. Department of Agriculture) grades, of food, **YM** 27
Uterus, **UB** 20, 140

VA mortgage

Vagina

VA mortgage, **YM** 100
Vacation(s), accommodation, **GT** 30 ; adventurous, **GT** 60 ; cancellation, **GT** 132 ; car insurance, **GT** 136 ; care of children of working mothers, **PY** 122 ; children's needs, **GT** 137 ; club, **GT** 21 ; definition, **GT** 17 ; educational, **GT** 79 ; family, **GT** 17 ; budgeting for, **GT** 21 ; first aid kit, **GT** 135 ; for the elderly, **GF** 82 ; for teenagers, **GT** 89 ; addresses, **GT** 141 ; healthful effect of, **GF** 70 ; imaginary, **GT** 126 ; immunization procedures, **GT** 133 ; medical precautions, **GT** 133 ; of the future, **GT** 14-15 ; once-in-a-lifetime, **GT** 91 ; packing for, **GT** 139 ; renting a home, **GT** 48 ; spending money, **GT** 130 ; sports, **GT** 61 ; through the ages, **GT** 6-9
Vacations, weekend, **GT** 105
Vacation Exchange Club, Inc., **GT** 59 ; party, **UT** 29
Vacuum cleaners, **UT** 58 ; **YM** 71
Vagina, **UB** 20 ; explanation of, to the young child, **TW** 52 ; deodorants, **DL** 78 ; **UB** 126 ;

Value(s)

discharge, **UB** 138; itching, **UB** 138; lubrication, in pregnancy, **SS** 133; muscles of, **SS** 134; size of, following childbirth, **SS** 134
Value(s), definition, **YM** 10; family, as guide to teenagers, **FT** 49
Valve, main shutoff, location, **FB** 47; radiator, use of, **FB** 140
Variety, antedote to boredom, **KS** 64
Variety meats, **FL** 48; **UT** 11; **YM** 28
Vas deferens, in male sterilization, **SS** 98
Vase, decoupage, **CF** 102; mosaic, **CF** 24, 25
Vasectomy, **SS** 98, 99; effect on the male, **SS** 100
Veganism, **FL** 76
Vegetables, as border for flower garden, **UT** 50; cooking times, **FL** 51; economy tips, **UT** 7; fresh, tips on buying and using, **YM** 33; home freezing, **FL** 59; midget, **UT** 51; preparation for cooking, **FL** 51; storage, **FL** 58 (table); supermarket substandard, **FL** 142
Vegetarian dishes, **FL** 143
Vegetarianism, **FL** 75
Veneered furniture, **HD** 137; repair, **UT** 21
Venereal disease, carriers, **SS** 143; cure of, **SS** 141; of long standing, detection of, **SS** 142; other than syphilis and gonorrhea, **SS** 143; risks of secrecy, **SS** 142; signs of, in woman, **SS** 140; suspected, **SS** 141; tests for, **SS** 141; transmission of infection, **SS** 142
Venetian blinds, **HD** 52
Ventilation, home system, **FB** 140
Vents, of heating system, **FB** 81
Venus de Milo, **DL** 8
Veterans' Administration, **FT** 133; **YM** 93
Victorian attitudes to love, **SS** 12-13
Victorian furniture style, **HD** 66
Vinyl floorings, **HD** 47; place mats, **UT** 30; wall coverings, **HD** 36; tiles, **HD** 36
Virginia, historic restoration, **GT** 105
Virginity, **SS** 73; **WM** 40
Visa, **GT** 103
Visiting manners, teaching to children, **UT** 48
Vitamins, **UB** 63; destruction by cooking, **FL** 37; dietary, **FL** 18; economic buying of, **YM** 140; fate of, in processing of food, **FL** 37, 39; food contents of 68 (chart); in cosmetics, **FL** 126; loss in freezing of meat, **FL** 64; malabsorption, through use of mineral oil preparations, **UB** 87; supplementation of flour, **FL** 72
Vitamin A, deficiency, effects, **FL** 134; foods containing, **FL** 20; supplementary, **FL** 75
Vitamins, B complex, **FL** 20; destruction in food processing, **FL** 37; for healthy hair, **DL** 57; in excess tea and coffee drinking, **UB** 83; B_{12}, **FL** 74, 77
Vitamin C, **FL** 21; daily requirement, **FL** 134; depletion by aspirin, **UB** 84; destruction in food processing, **FL** 37; massive doses against colds, **FL** 75; retention, in cooking vegetables, **FL** 51, 54
Vitamin D, **FL** 21, 75
Vitamin E, **FL** 21, 72, 134
Vitamin K, **FL** 21
Vizinczey, Stephen, *In Praise of Older Women*, **DL** 24
Vocational guidance, **PY** 54; counselor, work of, **PY** 131; for the single woman, **OY** 47
Voluntary nervous system, **UB** 40
Volunteer work, antedote to boredom, **KS** 73; for the single woman, **OY** 56; in personal inventory, **PY** 51; in relief of stress, **UB** 52-53
Vomiting of swallowed poison, **GF** 139, 140
Vulva, **UB** 18

Wage and Hour Office

Wage and Hour Office, **PY** 92
Wagon, covered, vacations, **GT** 72
Waistline, exercises for, **DL** 98-101
Walking, health value of, **DL** 107; **UB** 15, 98
Walking out, for the single woman, personal safety precautions, **OY** 143
Wallboard repairs, **FB** 101; studs, locating, **FB** 42, 43
Wall-hanging, macrame, **CF** 115
Wallpaper, **HD** 34; buying enough for the job, **HD** 28, 32; "chip-paper", **HD** 134; for table covering, **HD** 105; on doors, **HD** 99; prepasted, **HD** 36; treatment, of living-dining room, **HD** 130
Walls, coverings, **HD** 36; curtain, **HD** 100; decorating, **HD** 26; textures, **HD** 26; through the ages, **HD** 8-9; disguise of bad features, **HD** 134; measurement, for decorating, **HD** 32; mosaic, **CF** 25; outlet, replacement, **FB** 68-70; papering, **HD** 36; picture decorations, **HD** 110; repairs, **FB** 101; shelving, **HD**

Wampum belts

21 ; switch, replacement, **FB** 66, 67, 68 ; tiles, **HD** 36, 133
Wampum belts, **YM** 8
Ward Eight, mixing, **UT** 39
Wardrobe, revitalizing of, **OY** 118
Warehouse sales, **YM** 58
Warranty, shopping, definition, **YM** 56
Wartime, women's work in, **PY** 12-13
Warts, folk remedies for, **GF** 10
Washers, as table decoration, **HD** 105 ; faucet, replacement of, **FB** 50
Washing machines, buying of, **YM** 67
Wasp net, destruction, **UT** 60
Water, abroad, safety for drinking, **GT** 134 ; food content, **UB** 64 ; for pets, **UT** 11 ; hard, drying effect on skin, **DL** 32 ; home use, economy tips, **UT** 56 ; intake, during dieting, **FL** 137 ; pills, **UB** 91 ; pipes, lint blockage, **UT** 56 ; retention, and high blood pressure, **FL** 105 ; system, draining of, **FB** 130
Water-soluble bath oils, **DL** 75 ; paint, **HD** 28
Waterways, vacations on, **GT** 66
Wax. See also Stearic acid ; for candle making, **CF** 48 ; removal of hair, **DL** 75 ; 76
Weather, bad, driving in, **FB** 126
Weatherproofing of the home, **FB** 84
Weatherstripping, **FB** 85
Weaving, **CF** 8-9
Wedding, who pays for what ? **UT** 42-43
Weekend guests, care of, **UT** 26 ; vacations, **GT** 105
Weight. See also Obesity ; Reducing ; children's averages, **GF** 27 (table) ; control, after reducing diets, **FL** 90 ; correct for individual, **DL** 86 ; ideal, for men, **GF** 60 (chart)
Weight Watchers, **DL** 84
Welfare benefits, for the divorced woman, **OY** 136. See also Social Security benefits
Wet dreams, **GF** 44 ; **TW** 93
Where to Get Help for a Drug Problem, **FT** 132
Whistling toilet, repair of, **FB** 52
White lead, ingredient of olden-day cosmetics, **DL** 42
White water trips, **GT** 67
Whiteheads, **DL** 34

Whole World Handbook, The, **GT** 89
Wholegrain foods, **FL** 72, 135
Wick, for candle making, **CF** 48
Wickerwork, Madeira, **CF** 13
Widening of room, by decoration, **HD** 130
Widowed man, incidence, **OY** 22 (chart)
Widowed woman, the, **OY** 18 ; incidence, **OY** 22 (chart) ; occupation for, **OY** 18. See also Jobs
Widowed woman, remarriage incidence, **OY** 119 (chart) ; sense of purpose, **OY** 20 ; through the ages, **OY** 8-9
Widowhood, financial preparation for, **OY** 140
Wife, as husband's "business asset", **WM** 143 ; as lover, **SS** 18, 23, 30, 42 ; desire for independence, **FT** 125 ; enforced separation from husband, **OY** 130 ; of the alcoholic, supporting role, **FT** 92 ; of the business executive, **WM** 111 ; tired, **KS** 61 ; working, **PY** 96 ; during husband's unemployment, **FT** 38
Wigs, **DL** 58-59, 62
Wild and Scenic Rivers Authority, **GT** 46
Wilderness Society camping club, **GT** 46, 77
Wildlife reserves, weekend visits, **GT** 112
Will, making of, **OY** 140
Windjammer cruises, **GT** 65
Window boxes, **HD** 90
Windows, **HD** 49 ; basement, dressing, **HD** 55 ; bay, dressing, **HD** 53 ; casement, fixit jobs on, **FB** 93 ; cleaning tips, **UT** 58 ; dressing for privacy, **HD** 136 ; heightening effect, **HD** 55 ; kitchen, **HD** 132 ; panes, replacement, **FB** 96 ; periodic inspection, **FB** 133 ; picture, dressing, **HD** 49 ; screens, home repairs, **FB** 142, 143 ; stained glass, DIY, **HD** 54 ; sticking, **FB** 92 ; storm, **UT** 56 ; storm damage to, **FB** 95 ; traditional, dressing, **HD** 50 ; treatment, in "shaping" rooms, **HD** 130 ; unusual, dressing, **HD** 54 ; weatherstripping, **FB** 85 ; widening effect, **HD** 55
Windshield wipers, **UT** 60
Wine, matching food with, **UT**

Wine